Short Jabs to the Head

Also by Stephen Fleischman …

The Reporter

*A Red in the House: The Unauthorized Memoir
of S. E. Fleischman*

Moose in the city—Toronto 2000

Short Jabs to the Head

✦

Snapshots of History
2005–2007

Stephen Fleischman

iUniverse, Inc.
New York Lincoln Shanghai

Short Jabs to the Head
Snapshots of History 2005–2007

iUniverse books may be ordered through booksellers or by contacting:

iUniverse
2021 Pine Lake Road, Suite 100
Lincoln, NE 68512
www.iuniverse.com
1-800-Authors (1-800-288-4677)

Because of the dynamic nature of the Internet, any Web addresses or links contained in this book may have changed since publication and may no longer be valid.

The views expressed in this work are solely those of the author and do not necessarily reflect the views of the publisher, and the publisher hereby disclaims any responsibility for them.

ISBN: 978-0-595-46445-6 (pbk)
ISBN: 978-0-595-90741-0 (ebk)

Printed in the United States of America

For

Isly, Jordann and Wyatt

"I opened my eyes, saw the world—and I love it!"

—Wyatt Archer Mabb

Contents

Foreword

by
Eric Bercovici

In April 1945, Ardy Rooney witnessed one of the first joyous encounters between the American and Russian Armies on the banks of the Elbe. "You got the feeling of exuberance," Rooney wrote for *Stars and Stripes*, "a great new world opening up."

Also in 1945, Ella Winter, widow of the famed American muckraking journalist Lincoln Steffens and one of the few women to report on the war from inside Russia, wrote in the introduction to her book *I Saw The Russian People* that at General Dwight D. Eisenhower's final Press Conference of the war in Paris, he was asked, "Is there anything in your experience with the Russians that leads you to feel we can't co-operate with them perfectly?"

"On my level, nothing," Eisenhower replied. "I have found the individual Russian one of the friendliest persons in the world … I am convinced that they want peace and a chance to develop themselves the same as anyone else … The peace lies, when you get down to it, with all the peoples of the world."

Enter Harry Truman. Franklin Roosevelt's New Dealers were soon pushed aside by the new Truman administration and the political swing to the right had begun. By 1947, the Russians had been transformed into America's primary menace. Enter the Cold War. How easily administration officials could plant stories in the *New York Times* and then quote them as proof of truth. The first step in the death of journalism.

But not all journalists went along with this. There were some who still wrote the truth and quite a few of them paid a heavy professional price for it, both in print and on radio and television.

Steve Fleischman was one of the early News Documentary Film writer/director/producers. He spent thirty years in Network News, ten at CBS NEWS, where he worked with Fred Friendly on the Murrow-Friendly CBS REPORTS series, and then at ABC NEWS for twenty years where he had his own documentary unit that eventually merged with the ABC NEWS ClOSE-UP series. During that period he did special shows for ABC Chairman Leonard Goldenson, notably "The Long Childhood of Timmy" on the subject of retardation and "To All the World's Children", an hour documentary as a gift to UNICEF, the United Nations Children's Fund.

How he escaped the blacklist during these years is told in his memoir, *A Red in the House.*

Steve Fleischman traveled to over 30 countries, from the United States to Africa to South America to the Middle East to Europe and Asia and there interviewed those people who were making the news on all sides of the important issues. General William Westmoreland in Vietnam, Sylvanus Olympio, President of Togo, in Lomé, Malcolm X in New York City, João Goulart, shortly after his becoming President of Brazil, Jimmy Hoffa, Coretta King, Jacques Cousteau, Pablo Escobar of the Medellin Cocaine Cartel in Colombia, the list goes on and on.

As does Steve Fleischman, writing today about this sad time of criminal politics, timid journalism and little courage. He is among the last of the genuine American radicals, practically a vanished breed, a critical observer, unafraid to write about where we are and how we got stuck in this morass by what is now generally agreed the worst administration in the history of this country.

At a time when both politicians and most journalists can't bring themselves to even say "Liar" when describing the outrageous dishonesty so evident in the White House and environs, Steve Fleischman is not scared to use the F-word.

Fascism.

And he doesn't use it lightly.

Read this collection of his articles and you'll see why Steve Fleischman's point of view is so important. You won't hear it on the 6 o'clock news or read it in the vapid, self-serving press. This is real journalism by a real journalist. They don't make 'em like that anymore.

PART I
Jabs

Beware the Lessons of History

A little bit of history can be a dangerous thing.

To understand where we are now, let's be straight about where we've come from, where we'd been for a long time, and where we may be heading.

It might explain something about the price of sugar, the Iraq War, the hidden homeless in American, global warming and the rape of the environment.

This country was born in genocide. That cannot be denied, even by the Holocaust deniers. We had been practicing genocide against the Native American population since Christopher Columbus discovered America in 1492. (I remember playing "cowboys and Indians", as a kid)

The genocide ended, more or less, with the Wounded Knee Massacre of the Dakota Sioux in 1890. According to Ward Churchill, an eminent authority and professor of ethnic studies at the University of Colorado, the North American Indian population went from an estimated 12 million in 1500 to barely 237,000 in 1900, "a vast genocide … the most sustained on record."

The remnants of the Native American nations that once inhabited this continent are now mostly scattered in the general population. Some still languish on the so-called reservations. The way we handle our embarrassment about it, today, is by throwing the people on the reservations, who claim to be Indians, some gambling franchises, mainly run by the mafia.

All of this notwithstanding, there was always a democratic streak running through our people. It came from the colonists who populated America. They rejected the old order in Europe from which they had fled. They wanted freedom, particularly religious freedom and they found it here. Their freedom gave rise, eventually, to the Bill of Rights in our Constitution.

But at the time, it was a short hop and a skip from genocide to slavery.

The plantation system grew with the speed of sugar cane in the British Caribbean. The English found a cash crop to fuel their Industrial Revolution. But they had a labor problem. Plantations need cheap labor and lots of it. The plantation owners had the vision to see that they could profit three ways from the "triangular trade" between Europe, Africa and the Americas. The commercial hunting of black skins was profitable. The Portuguese became proficient at it, learning from black African tribesmen who have been enslaving each other for centuries. In the slave trade that flourished between West Africa and the plantations of America, skin color and slavery became linked.

The slave population of the Americas reached 33,000 in 1700, nearly three million in 1800 and peaked at over six million in 1850. Handling so many hostile and resistant people became unwieldy. In the United States, the clash between slave states and Free states wasn't solved by the Missouri Compromise.

We had to fight a civil war to find out that slavery was not the right system for capitalism. Why own your worker as a chattel? That's wasteful.

Under a free labor system, you pay your worker a wage (that represents only a part payment for the value he produces). You have only to extract the surplus value that the worker contributes to the making of the product. You call it profit and say it is derived from entrepreneurial skill, reward for taking risks, from the machinery, the land, or other such gibberish. Once you extract the surplus value the worker creates, let him be free to go his own way and the devil take the hindmost. There is always a supply of fresh labor to be had.

That's not the end of the story. What happens is that eventually, the worker wises up and starts to demand the full value of his work, or maybe settle for a larger slice of the pie. That's when the fur begins to fly. It's called the class struggle.

Throughout economic history that struggle has gone on. It's an old, old fight between the haves and the have-nots. It pushes capital on to heights of glory, monopoly and war. We're in such a period right now.

We need to keep production high and labor costs low to keep the system afloat, they tell us. The EPA notwithstanding, production and profits trump the environment. Take a look at us now. Shop until you drop, the propaganda organs shout. "But with what?" asks the underpaid and the unemployed.

The class struggle will go on. One day, it will reach a turning point. With computers and digital technology, a planned economy is not only more feasible but inevitable in a future socialist society.

It took capitalism four hundred years to hone its skills. It's a trial and error process. The system served its purpose and is now ready to leave the stage of history, or "dig its own grave" if you prefer Marx's expression. There's a new one waiting in the wings. Only been around about a century. Made a couple of mistakes but learning. Has its own theme song:

(sung to the tune of "The Internationale")

Arise, you prisoners of starvation!
Arise, you wretched of the earth!
For justice thunders condemnation:
A better world's in birth!
No more tradition's chains shall bind us,
Arise you slaves, no more in thrall!
The earth shall rise on new foundations:
We have been nought, we shall be all!
'Tis the final conflict,
Let each stand in his place.
The international working class
Shall be the human race ...

The Bee Sting

Don't mess with nature!

It may not be a nuclear war or global warming that brings us down, but the mysterious disappearance of the honey bee. We've been messing with nature since Adam plucked the first piece of fruit off the apple tree.

The New York Times, on Feb 23rd, reported on a beekeeper named David Bradshaw in Visalia, California who got the shock of his life when he opened his boxes one morning and found half of his 100 million bees missing. His bees had been pollinating the almond crop in the Central Valley, the world's largest almond producing area.

The honey bee, *apis mellifera,* is the most commonly domesticated species in the United States and is used not only for producing honey, but more importantly for pollinating crops. Hence, the consternation when it was discovered recently that bees in 24 states across the country were mysteriously disappearing. The bees leave their hives to seek pollen and nectar and in the process pollinate the blossoms of the crop. But these bees never return to the hive and the colony becomes defunct. The phenomenon has been given the name, "Colony Collapse Disorder". The scientists are scratching their heads. They don't understand what's happening here. At least, not yet.

Apis mellifera provides pollination for more than 90 commercial crops grown throughout the United States. Tens of billions of bees are involved in "migratory" pollination, going from crop to crop. The value of the agricultural output of these bee pollinated crops is estimated at more than 14 billion dollars annually. They include everything from oranges in Florida to apples in Pennsylvania to blueberries in Maine and cranberries in Massachusetts, to name a few.

Why are the bees ditching their hives and going astray? Are they on strike for a bigger piece of the honey pie?

"We are extremely alarmed," said Diana Cox-Foster, the professor of Entomology at Penn State University and one of the leading members of a specially convened colony-collapse disorder working group. "It is one of the most alarming insect diseases ever to hit the US and it has the potential to devastate the US beekeeping industry."

Too bad for the beekeeping industry, but what are we going to eat if our fruits and vegetables don't get pollinated? No seeds, no plants, no food.

US Department of Agriculture: don't just sit there. Do something! The delicate filaments of the web of life are being torn. We know that all life is inter-connected. We learned that when we studied Ecology in first grade. ("… and the thigh bone's connected to the hip bone …")

Maybe these honey bees don't like the idea of having their hives put in boxes, stacking the boxes up on flat-bed trucks and "shleping" them around the country, pollinating strange fruit, doing "the man's" work who then goes and steals their honey. It may do something to their psyche.

Investigators of "Colony Collapse Disorder" found a new set of symptoms. The few bees left inside the hive were carrying "a tremendous number of pathogens"—every known bee virus as well as fungal infections. Even "robber bees", the wax moth and the hive beetle are afraid to enter the hives to steal the honey.

What we have here may be another example of capitalist exploitation gone awry. The big commercial beekeeping operations care more about production and profits than they do about the welfare of the bees. Corporate operators are trying to extract too much of the surplus value created by the bees. It seems they are able to do that with people but not with bees.

To save our food supply—and our lives, the corporate bee exploiters better go back to the drawing board and bone up on economics. The "invisible hand" (laissez faire) is not going to make it in these circumstances.

There are two roads they can take. Go back to small commodity production or advanced technology. If they can devise a new technology for pollinating crops, like giant fans that can blow pollen around and get it to land on the billions of blossoms, that might do the trick. Then the bees can go back to doing what they do best—providing honey for us.

The other alternative might be better. Break up these giant corporations that have assumed the status of people and get away with murder (literally). They are more interested in arms production and provoking wars, which are much more profitable than pollinating crops. Corporations are chartered by the states. If they don't do the job they are chartered to do, their charters can be revoked. That's how they were originally set up and that's the law. The state giveth and the state can taketh away. But have you ever heard of one charter being revoked? Not lately. They have grown too powerful to be messed with. However, it can be done.

We can go back to small commodity production. Mom and Pop operations, as we used to have. The bees will go back to work for us as they always did. The Queen just has to say the word.

Who's Afraid of Single Payer?

Who's afraid of the single payer health plan, otherwise known as National Health Insurance?

Big Pharma and the medical establishment, that's who—because "single payer" is the big bad wolf that's huffing and puffing and is about to blow their house down. And it's a big house, bloated by excess profits, government subsidies and sheer theft of the people's money.

To paraphrase our former President, Richard Nixon, "you're not going to have America's healthcare system to kick around forever."

Health Insurance has been a political football in this country for decades. It's been on every politician's laundry list, in one form or another, in every election. There have been employer plans; there have been government plans; city, state and federal plans. It's been brought up again and again in every State of the Union address, year after year. Despite all the talk and attention by both parties, census figures show that a record 46.6 million Americans, including 8.3 million children, have no health insurance at all, at a time when the cost of health care has gone through the roof. How can they afford to see a doctor or fill a prescription?

Are we going to go on talking the talk and getting ripped off by Big Insurance forever? Why can't we have what every other industrialized nation in the world enjoys—some form of national health insurance?

That may be the first question some Democratic Congressman or Senator may ask now that they have a majority in both houses of Congress—but I doubt it.

A look back at the endless squabble over health care in this country will reveal where this timidity comes from.

It all began with the bug-a-boo of "Socialized Medicine" raised by the American Medical Association after World War II when they saw their "fee-for-service" system being threatened. The system was: You go to the doctor, you get a service and you pay a fee; and that's the way they wanted to keep it, by God!

But after the war, something new was blowin' in the wind. People like Henry Kaiser, the auto maker and ship builder, came up with a Health Maintenance Organization (HMO) for his employees. You pay a small monthly fee, you get your entire medical and hospital needs free of any other charges.

The city of New York jumped right in with HIP (Health Insurance Plan of Greater New York), a pre-paid health plan for city employees.

"Socialized medicine!" screamed the AMA. Physicians and surgeons manned the battle stations. Many saw their seven figure incomes taking flight.

Other HMOs mushroomed around the country. And then, in 1965, President Lyndon Johnson made "medical care for the aged" part of his *Great Society* package. We know it today as *Medicare*. Then came *Medicaid*, medical care for the indigent. The flood gates were opened. For the first time, huge amounts of government money started pouring into the health care system.

The insurance industry knew a good thing when they saw it. Organized medicine, the AMA and its state and county medical societies, did not—paralyzed by the fear of government intrusion.

Insurance companies relished the enormous cash flow of government money emanating from *Medicare* and *Medicaid* and other government programs like *Champus,* medical coverage for servicemen and their families.

Insurance companies set up their own private plans, yes, HMOs, to sop up all that loose cash. They turned pre-paid plans into their opposite—not "socialized medicine" for the people but corporate welfare for the insurance companies. Through the years, they increased premiums and cut services, raking in billions in profits instead of providing not-for-profit medical services to their subscribers. The doctors allowed themselves to be co-opted and blind-sided. They allowed the pre-paid plans to get away from them. Their fear of "socialized medicine" dimmed their vision.

Instead of "socialized medicine" the doctors got privatized sweatshops where some doctors can't make medical decisions without the approval of an HMO bureaucrat. Managed care became mismanaged medicine.

The epitome of outrage was Hillary and Bill Clinton's opportunistic brainstorming of a National Health Plan in 1992. They devised a government health plan they knew would never work. They dangled it before the nation. They were too politically sophisticated not to know they were playing right into the hands of the insurance companies.

The Clintons set the national health care movement back a generation. Now, Hillary Clinton is running for president in 2008. What's her health care program? More of the same. Single payer? No way.

The current health insurance system violates the very essence of the insurance principle—the widest coverage for the least cost. The larger the pool, the more efficient the system.

In the current US system, there are literally tens of thousands of different, and overlapping, health care organizations generating a blizzard of paperwork in an administrative wilderness creating enormous waste—thousands, if not millions of people pushing paper around. They are driving doctors, trying to do a job, up the wall with the different forms needed to be completed in order to get paid, to say nothing of patients fighting their way through a jungle of obstacles trying to get the health care they need.

A single payer system would eliminate all that.

One administrator or "payer"—yes, a government supervised agency, would collect all health care fees and pay out all health care costs. In a single payer system, all hospitals, doctors and other health care providers would bill one entity for their services. Every US citizen would be covered. It's been done successfully in most "civilized" countries. Why not here?

US health care is in crisis, today. The system just isn't working, for anybody, except, maybe the health insurance industry and their HMOs that are siphoning off whopping profits. But doctors aren't happy. Patients are burdened more and more with increasing co-payments. Health care costs continue to skyrocket. And 47 million people remain uninsured. Sooner, if not later, the system will crash. Must we wait for that to happen?

Is Bush Creating the Perfect Storm?

With outsourcing and downsizing and factory closings, and digital communications made easy and cheap, both blue-collar and white-collar jobs started flying off to that nirvana of capital, the enticing venue of the rock bottom wage, making that giant sucking sound that Ross Perot once spoke of.

The industrial core of this country is being hollowed out.

Right now, we're having another great drive of corporatism in the United States. President Eisenhower tried to warn us about it before he left office by calling it "the Military Industrial complex". Benito Mussolini, the former dictator of Italy defined it in another way. He called "Corporatism" the interlocking of government and corporate power otherwise known as Fascism.

It might do us some good to look back and learn some lessons of history.

The first great drive of corporatism hit the nation during the "Robber Baron" period, the late 19th and early 20th Century. So-called "captains of industry", Rockefeller, Carnegie, Morgan, Gould, Vanderbilt, to name a few, started carving up the country, stealing what they could from the government, the land and the laboring classes.

There were also some sung and unsung heroes of the day that appeared on the scene during that period intent on protecting those laboring classes from the depredations of capitalist exploitation. They were engaged in what is called union organizing.

Although trade unions and guilds of various kinds existed before the Civil War, with the end of slavery, wage labor more appropriately met the needs of industry. The union movement became more militant. There were the *Molly Maguires* in the Pennsylvania coalfields, the *National Labor Union* and the *Knights of Labor,* the first of the national unions. By the 1880s they gave way to the *America Federation of Labor (AFL),* its first president, Sam Gompers, who hung in that job for thirty-eight years until his death in 1924.

The internal conflicts in the labor movement were fought over policy, bitter and uncompromising. Sam Gompers certainly was one of the protagonists. His antagonist and nemesis was Eugene V. Debs. The sticking point—should the labor movement restrict itself to economic issues, wages and working conditions—or extent its influence into politics, Socialist and otherwise?

Horace Greeley, who founded the New York Tribune in 1841, was very interested in Socialist ideas and published articles by Karl Marx in his newspaper. Over the years, many of these ideas—Marx's incisive analysis of Capitalism—seeped into the heads of some union leaders. A Socialist America was not unthinkable to many in those days.

"Big Bill" Haywood, blind in one eye but a man with vision nonetheless, a veteran of many bloody strikes in Western coal country, became a founding member, in 1905, of the *International Workers of the World (IWW)* also known as "the Wobblies." Haywood believed in "One Big Union" organized along industrial lines and had this to say at the opening convention:

"Fellow workers! This is the Continental Congress of the Working Class! We are here to confederate the workers of this country ... to take control of the machinery of production and distribution without regard to capitalist masters."

Another Wobblie, Joe Hill, a songwriter, itinerant laborer and union organizer, led the dockworkers' strike in San Pedro where he was arrested on trumped up charges and found guilty of a murder he didn't commit. His fellow workers and comrades organized a major campaign to exonerate Hill but all efforts failed. Before his execution by firing squad on November 19, 1915, Joe Hill wrote to Big Bill Haywood:

"Good-bye Bill: I die like a true rebel. Don't waste any time mourning, organize!"

Labor organizer, Vincent St. John, Socialist, and for a time, head of the IWW, was shadowed by the Pinkertons, stalked by gunmen, had a price on his head, was arrested and charged with crimes he didn't commit, and was condemned by the mainstream press as a murderer. But his colleagues and comrades called him "the Saint".

One of those who stood above the crowd, Eugene V. Debs, started as a railroad fireman, organized the *American Railway Union (ARU)*, led the infamous Pullman strike in Chicago where Federal troops were used to bust the union. Debs ran for President of the United States on the American Socialist Party ticket in 1900, 1904, 1908, 1912 and 1920, the last race from Atlanta Prison where he was jailed again for union activity. Debs was a great communicator, a spellbinding orator. The slogan on his campaign poster in 1920 read: "From Atlanta Prison to the Whitehouse!" He received nearly one million votes that year.

In 1925, writer Alfred Hayes wrote a poem about Joe Hill that was put to music by Earl Robinson in 1936; thus, later generations were inspired by Joe's story. This is the first verse:

I dreamed I saw Joe Hill last night,
Alive as you and me.
Says I "But Joe, you're ten years dead"
"I never died" said he,
"I never died" said he.

So—what have we learned from all this that can help stop Bush and his administration from riding the ship of state into the perfect storm?

Well—let's listen again to what Joe Hill said to Big Bill Haywood before he died:

"Don't mourn for me, organize!"

Sounds good, doesn't it? But those old fashioned ideas now seem romantic and quaint. They won't work today. With union membership down to 13%, we can't count on organized labor for much leadership, hard as they try.

We have a new set of circumstances, today. And we need a new strategy and tactics to deal with it.

We have a growing pool, more of a roaring river of unskilled, mostly foreign born working class and underclass residents in this country, some citizens, some not. We have college graduates with no place to go. The formerly good jobs are now overseas. We have evaporating purchasing power as those good jobs disappear. With rising technology, the productivity of labor skyrockets, but the ability to buy the products we make or import plummets.

Bush says our economy is sound. Yes, for whom? Not for the working class, the under-employed or the unemployed. Bush wants to institutionalize his tax cuts for the rich, has come up with a new military budget of more than 400 billion and, at the same time, wants to cut social spending. Would you call that rational?

We're burdened with more than a military-industrial complex. We have a militarized nation. Still, the day is not far off when we'll be forced out of Iraq as we were out of Vietnam. Our economy, despite Bush's assurances, is being guided by a quivering invisible hand.

Bush is setting us up for the perfect storm.

Where are the Debs' and the Haywoods and the Hills and "the Saints" of today, now that we really need them?

Oil: Too Valuable to Burn

The Shah of Iran, America's puppet monarch in the good old days before the Iranian revolution of 1979, is reputed to have said, "Oil is too valuable to burn".

Iran sat on one of the largest pools of oil in the Middle East. It whet the appetites of all the imperial powers still functioning at the time. The nation that had a leg up, of course, was Great Britain. They had the Anglo-Iranian Oil Company. After World War II they had converted their coal burning Naval fleet to oil, so they needed plenty of it.

Britain's major source of oil was threatened after World War II when Dr. Mohammad Mossadeq, the only truly democratic leader in Iranian history, was elected Premier in 1951. The first thing he did was to nationalize the Anglo-Iranian Oil Company. This outraged the British but they were too inept to do anything about it, themselves, so they called their ally, the USA, and begged them to get their oil company back for them.

America was eager to help. Serve an ally and maybe serve yourself a piece of the pie. They assigned the job to Kermit Roosevelt, son of Theodore, a big wheel in the newly formed CIA. He masterminded the CIA coup that got rid of Mossadeq.

Kermit bought off Iranian officials with huge sums of money, organized demonstrations by rival groups provoking conflict and violence in the streets over Mossadeq policy. It took several attempts by Kermit, but he was eventually successful in forcing Mossadeq out. It was the CIA's first big adventure in covert operations and set the pattern for its modus operandi for years to come.

Kermit re-privatized the oil company for the British and reinstalled the Shah on his Peacock Throne. It was 1953, and there he reigned until 1979 when he was booted again, this time by the Ayatollah Khumeini who also took 44 Americans hostage.

"Oil is too valuable to burn," said the Shah from exile in Italy. What did he mean by that? When pushed, the Shah elaborated. "There are more important uses for oil than burning it to produce energy, for God's sake!"

"There's a limited amount of crude petroleum in the earth," he said. "Oil is used for making plastics and thousands of other products made by petrochemicals which is oil." He knew what he was talking about.

"Oil is too valuable to burn," the Shah reiterated. "When we run out, what will we do? Fight each other for the last drop?"

He got it right again.

War is the greatest despoiler of the environment and depletor of petroleum products. Imagine how much hi-octane aviation gasoline it takes to fly one bomber to drop one bomb on Baghdad, say from a base in Diego Garcia in the Indian ocean; then multiply that by "shock and awe" and take the square root of the thousands of Humvees and Abrams and Sherman tanks and troop carriers that need to be supplied each day times 365 days times 3 years. Any wonder then that the price of gas is three dollars a gallon at the pump and the profits of the oil companies have gone through the roof!

And with China getting into the act, promising its people a chicken in every pot and two cars in every garage, what is a little nation like the USA to do?

Where is Mossadeq now that we really need him?

Confrontation?

Rejoice! Congress seems to have come to life!

The President has drawn his line in the sand and a Senator has crossed it!

"We will not go along with a partisan fishing expedition aimed at honorable public servants," President Bush said in a last ditch effort to keep his manipulator, Karl Rove, and his former attorney, Harriet Miers, from being questioned under oath in a Congressional hearing. They would be grilled on the scandal that's been hanging over the Justice Department, and particularly Alberto Gonzales, the Attorney General, about the dismissal of eight US Federal Attorneys allegedly for political purposes.

Senator Patrick Leahy, D-VT., chairman of the Senate Judiciary Committee, is the man who stepped across that line in the sand and threatened to send out subpoenas for Rove, Miers and their aides if they didn't appear voluntarily. "I want testimony under oath. I'm sick and tired of getting half-truths on this," said Leahy. "Testimony should be on the record and under oath. That's the formula for true accountability ... it is not helpful to be telling the Senate how to do our investigation or to prejudge its outcome."

Rep. John Conyers, Jr., Democrat of Michigan, chairman of the House Judiciary Committee doesn't want anyone like the President telling him how to do his investigation, either. He is also preparing subpoenas for Rove and Miers to get their sworn testimony in the House inquiry.

It's great to see Congress, the House and the Senate, the voice, the force and the soul of the people's democracy, get some spine and confront an executive branch gone wild.

The executive branch has gone wild before. Warren Harding took his lumps at Teapot Dome and Richard Nixon at Watergate—probably the granddaddy of Congressional confrontations with executive privilege.

Senator Sam Ervin, self-styled "country lawyer", Democrat of North Carolina, became chairman of the Senate Select Committee investigating Watergate and went head-to-head with President Richard M. Nixon.

It was a "third rate burglary" during the Nixon re-election campaign in 1972 that kicked off the confrontation. A group of plumbers (they fix leaks) operating from the basement of the White House broke into the Democratic National Headquarters that happened to be located in the Watergate Office Building in Washington. They were trying to bug the place to spy on Democratic election strategy—and they got caught, red handed.

The Congressional investigation of the event and its cover-up didn't take place until a year later. In the interim, Nixon was reelected. After three months of testimony by Nixon's motley crew, subpoenaed before the Ervin Committee in 1973, Nixon yelled "uncle" and resigned rather than face impeachment.

Republicans have no monopoly on executive chutzpah. Welcome to the ranks, FDR!

In 1937, when the Supreme Court kept overturning some of his New Deal measures, President Franklin Delano Roosevelt found a loophole he thought he could squeeze through. Simply pack the Court. He wanted the authority to appoint new members to the Supreme Court who would be more apt to vote his way. There is nothing in the Constitution that says the Supreme Court has to be limited to nine members. So Roosevelt put through the Judiciary Reorganization Bill of 1937, which was signed into law, post haste. It gave him the power to appoint an extra Supreme Court Justice for every sitting Justice over the age of 70 and a half. That would get him three or four more, enough for keeping his measures from being overturned. Why not twelve or fourteen justices? Nine is not a magic number.

Before Roosevelt could take advantage of the feint, a howl went up across the country and rippled through Congress. Eventually, Roosevelt gave up the ghost, and we went back to the traditional 9 (count'em) 9 Supreme Court justices—one Chief Justice and eight Associates. (who will probably be used to save Bush's bacon in the current bru-ha-ha, if it gets to court.)

Right now, we have a plethora of confrontations. With hearings brewing in both the House and Senate, some representatives are also considering legislation that would tie funding for military operations in Iraq and Afghanistan to a September 2008 deadline for troop withdrawal. There are also votes in the offing on opposing Bush's plans to increase US troop levels in Iraq. And it looks like a number of Republicans are being swept along with the tide.

Witnesses are sworn when they testify before a Congressional Investigating Committee as a way of getting them to tell the truth.

Raise your right hand.

"I do solemnly swear and attest that the testimony I will give shall be the truth, the whole truth and nothing but the truth, under penalty of perjury (so help me God)"

A simple statement. It carries a lot of weight.

President Bush has offered Rove's and Miers' testimony to Congress behind closed doors, without an oath and without a transcript. What is he afraid of?

"We could meet at the local pub to have that kind of gathering," said Rep. John Conyers, D-Detroit, chairman of the House Judiciary Committee.

Would you like to see Karl Rove and Harriet Miers go before Congressional Committees—sworn or unsworn?

Like a Soldier

When you're wounded and left on Afghanistan's plains,
And the women come out to cut up what remains,
Jest roll to your rifle and blow out your brains
An' go to your Gawd like a soldier.

Rudyard Kipling knew what he was talking about when he wrote that verse. As a chronicler of the British Empire in its declining years, he foreshadowed the coming of America's Empire in his advice to the British soldier. But we know that a better way to support our troops is to bring them home now. Who would want to be the last soldier to die in the Iraq war?

It seems that the Bush Administration is beginning to admit what we have known for some time—that the war in Iraq is already lost. So should we continue to "blow out our brains" as the British did on Afghanistan's plains, or should we cut and run as we did in Vietnam, although a bit too late.

The Bush war party is being gored by the horns of a dilemma. Some members of the establishment are calling for a reduction of forces, maybe 30 thousand or so, to ward off stinging defeat in the upcoming Congressional elections. Other factions in the Administration, mainly the neocons, are calling for the addition of more troops to do what some say should have been done in the first place—send in overwhelming force and do what Colin Powell so graphically described in the first Gulf War, "surround the enemy, cut it off and kill it." Unfortunately for him (and for us) he didn't take his own advice and went along with the Rumsfeld concept of doing this war "on the cheap".

Not quite so cheap, as it turned out. The theft of 18 billion dollars, here and there, doesn't seem like much compared with the 1 trillion or 2 trillion the war has cost our hardy taxpayers thus far, depending on who's calculating the damage. How many school lunches or health insurance policies would that buy?

When will we get out of Iraq? Not until we're kicked out, it seems. This is getting more and more like déjà vu all over again. Bush has given up his mantra, "stay the course", but he has not quit his other bright saying, "When the Iraqis stand up, we'll stand down". The estimates change almost daily. "Now the Iraqis are standing up ... now they're standing down ... now they're being decimated by the insurgents ... well, some of them are standing up, no ... I mean standing down ...

Meanwhile, judging from the nightly news clips, our troops seem to be running around in circles in the most dangerous place in the world—busting into people's houses, intimidating children, terrorizing women, and harassing their men, killing some of them, looking for terrorists and insurgents. A great way to win the hearts and minds of the people; a cliché they still talk about. But the resistance goes on, the way it did in Algiers when Algeria finally dumped the French.

"Take up the White Man's burden—Send forth the best ye breed ..." said Kipling. That's what Bush thought he was doing when he sent young men like Cindy Sheehan's son, Casey, into battle in Iraq in order to bring freedom and free enterprise (not for the Iraqis but for Halliburton, Bechtel and Boeing) into this *Saddam-ized* country.

Now that Bush's military adventurism is falling apart, the news of it is busting out all over. Even the popular German news magazine, *Der Spiegel,* heralded the US loss of the Iraq War, this week, under a banner headline "Power and Lies".

Now, even Republicans are beginning to speak up. Pennsylvania Congressman Curt Weldon, a member of the House Armed Services Committee, once a hawk, is now asking for a timetable to bring the troops home. Other dissident Republicans are following suit. Rep. Christopher Shays of Connecticut favors a timeline for troop withdrawals, New Jersey's Tom Kean, Jr., running for the Senate called for Rumsfeld's resignation and said Bush had made "horrendous mistakes", Pat Tiberi of Ohio called for new leadership at the Pentagon, Sen. Lindsey Graham called Iraq "a mess", and so it goes. They all want to put some distance between George Bush and their candidacy. A looming election has magical powers.

To distract his right-wing constituency from the truth, Bush has given the so-called Iraqi government a "timeline"—a series of tasks for establishing security that they must complete in a period of time before the occupying troops can leave. Another gimmick. If they haven't been able to accomplish these tasks before having a timeline, they're not going to be any better off with one.

What are we going to think of next? Major General J.D. Thurman, senior commander of US forces in Baghdad came up with a good answer—do what's right for the country. Right now, the Iraqis are so splintered, it would be harder to get them back together again than it would be to get Humpty Dumpty back on the wall. So why not let them fight it out and if they decide to split into three regions, Sunni, Shia and Kurds, so be it.

Meanwhile, the resistance grows. Everyone waits expectantly for that tipping point when Grand Ayatollah al Sistani tips his turban and the Shia join the Sunni insurgency against the occupiers—the end of the beginning.

If it can be said that Osama bin Laden was the "Gunga Din" of 9/11 (carrying water for al Qaeda), there will come a time when George W. Bush will have to say to Osama, "You're a better man than I am, Gunga Din".

Enemy of the People

✦

(with apologies to Henrik Ibsen)

"… the strongest man in the world is the man who stands most alone," so said Henrik Ibsen, Norwegian playwright, in his 1882 work concerned with the "irrational tendencies of the masses and the hypocritical and corrupt nature of the political system that they support." Sounds like the United States today.

An enemy of the people is someone who commits a crime against humanity, who violates the Geneva Convention, who breaks the International Laws of War, who disregards the Fourth Amendment of the Bill of Rights in our Constitution, who secretly has American citizens under surveillance, who lies his people into war.

Headline: "Arab Democracy, a US Goal, Falters," The New York Times, Dubai, United Arab Emirates, April 9—

You can't bring democracy to a people at the point of a gun. Everybody knows that. But is there another factor at play here?

It's not just piano-playing Condolessa Rice, our Secretary of State, who has it: it's all the other sages, neocons and otherwise, working at the White House and Pentagon who have it; it's endemic in the mainstream media and, to a certain degree, in the general population. You can call it the "hegemonic attitude" or simply, the imperialist mindset.

There are those who think of this nation not just as policeman to the world. It goes deeper than that. A "droit du Seigneur" frame of mind? What's yours is mine; the right of the first night—you exist to supply us. We have the right to take the world's resources so that we can live in the style to which we have become accustomed.

They also call it "globalization". Thomas Friedman, New York Times columnist, says the world is flat. Yes, it's been flattened with a knockout punch—the proliferation of free trade agreements.

The attitude developed a head of steam in the Robber Baron period when Teddy Roosevelt and his Rough Riders charged up San Juan Hill, got rid of the Spanish and took over the territory. Never mind the Cuban's own revolt taking place at the time. Those in the US government, with imperialist mindset, thought they could do the same thing in other vulnerable Spanish colonies like Puerto Rico and the Philippines. There was no talk of democracy then. The quality of greed cannot be tempered. It's the system, Stupid! Capitalism leads to Monopoly, to Imperialism and War.

That frame of mind goes back to the days of our glory when we had a thriving democracy and the American Dream was the Holy Grail and we wished it upon everybody in the world.

President Woodrow Wilson said we joined the Allies in World War I to save the world for democracy. It was really about grabbing natural resources and markets.

In 1953, we saved Britain's oil for them by stopping the British-Iranian Oil Co. from being nationalized. The US government sent in Kermit Roosevelt to do the job. He, handily, got rid of Muhammad Mossadeq, Iran's first and perhaps only democratic leader. It was the beginning of a tactic used frequently by the US, known henceforth as "covert action". Britain, ever grateful, helped us out in Iraq.

Today, it would be a stretch to think of the United States as policeman to the world; disciplinarian would be more like it. We can't allow Iran to have a nuclear weapon. We can't let Hugo Chavez of Venezuela cast his Socialist spell over Latin America. We can't tolerate Hamas leading the Palestinian government. What's a struggling monopoly-capitalist nation to do?

Can we only allow democracy in other countries when they elect puppet governments acceptable to "us"? Look at what's happening in Iraq. They had an election that we forced on them and the Iraqis elected a government of Islamic fundamentalists. Is that fair? Our Secretary of State made a trip to Iraq to try to get the elected president to resign. That's democracy in action.

President George W. Bush now has his laser gaze trained on Iran. He'd like to make a return visit, in the spirit of Kermit Roosevelt. Is that country, too, about to be democratized?

Small, vulnerable, countries are looking around to see what others have done to protect themselves from this wave of democracy—like North Korea—the third spoke in the Bush "axis of evil".

The devilish Kim Jong Il has managed to develop for himself a few primitive nuclear bombs—not much, but enough to make things uncomfortable for its neighboring countries, South Korea and Japan, nations friendly to the US. Bush has been notably silent on the subject of North Korea lately. He's turned his attention to more feasible game.

But how feasible? Iranian President Mahmoud Ahmadinejad, a darling of the mullahs, has been enriching uranium with a new process called "P-2", which he swears is for peaceful purposes, but which will also speed up the production of a nuclear weapon. Furthermore, it has been reported that Iran has lined up 40,000 suicide bombers ready to attack Britain, Israeli and US interests around the world. These will be unleashed should Iran's nuclear facilities be disturbed by a shock and awe aerial bombardment, even if done with precision and care by US forces to lessen the amount of collateral damage. It has also been reported that the use of tactical nuclear weapons is one of the options on the table in consideration of such a bombardment.

Will the American people, again, take this attack on their life, liberty and the pursuit of happiness, lying down, as they did in the strike on Iraq? I don't think so.

In that case, will the strongest man in the world please stand up! The only one I can see from here is Cindy Sheehan—and she stands most alone.

Havanas

What this country needs is a good 25-cent cigar and a lesson in political economy.

If you can explain the Theory of Surplus Value clearly enough, you'd make a Communist out of every working class American. Stop right there! Don't go reaching for your copy of Marx's *Das Kapital!*

The question is simply this. Do you want your labor power stolen from you—or any part of the value of your labor "taken" by somebody else? That's what happens when you work for someone producing a commodity that he sells in the marketplace.

I know you're going to challenge this because you're in a union and are getting a fair wage for your work. And you keep getting raises and you feel good about it, and you love your boss, and you think you are getting paid fully for the work you do for him. Well, think again.

And the first thing you should think of is, "How is he making a profit and staying in business?" That's the rub and here is where you have to get a little help from your friend, Karl.

Face it—your labor is producing the boss' profit—not his factory, not his machines, not his land, not his entrepreneurial skills in the market-place. Yes, some say he deserves a reward for risking his capital. Okay, but why should it come out of your hide? It's your labor and the labor of your fellow workers, from which surplus value is derived. And the surplus value you produce is his profit.

Marx put it this way in his theory of exploitation: "living labour is able to create and conserve more value than it costs the employer to buy; which is exactly the economic reason why the employer buys it. That's how he preserves and augments the value of the capital at his command. Thus, the surplus-labour is *unpaid* labour appropriated by employers in the form of work-time. Human labour is the only source of net new economic value, and that's his profit." And it's coming out of *YOU*.

You're okay with that? Then stop reading, right now.

For those who are game to explore a little more, we can dig deeper, not only into Marx, but those economists who preceded him like Adam Smith, John Stuart Mill, David Ricardo and others, the classical economists of capitalism who came up with the concepts of "the free market" and the "invisible hand."

In 1776, Adam Smith published his great work, *An Inquiry into the Nature and Causes of the Wealth of Nations* in which he defined the transition from feudalism to the incoming capitalist system via the industrial revolution that began in late 18th Century England. He examined in detail the consequences of economic freedom, the role of self-interest, division of labor, markets and the international implications of a laissez-faire economy. He made an important contribution to the understanding of capitalism and how it worked, which Marx studied assiduously at the British Museum.

In 1867, just about a century after *Wealth of Nations*, Karl Marx published his own work, *Das Kapital*, or "Capital", in which he defined the transition from capitalism to the inevitable next stage, the incoming socialist system, where the means of production are in the hands of the society as a whole instead of owned by individuals or corporate entities.

Adam Smith tried to demonstrate how self-interest (free enterprise, rugged individualism) produces the most efficient use of resources in a nation's economy. To underscore his laissez-faire convictions, Smith argued that social control of markets are ineffectual compared to uncontrolled market forces.

Marx knocked some of Smith's theories into a cocked hat. He proved that the "free market" wasn't free and that the "invisible hand" of the market, instead of maintaining economic stability, led the system into cycles of boom and bust. The clincher was his theory of surplus value that exposed the "profit" system as the villain of the piece. Marx pointed to the entire capitalist class as an exploitative entity, and to capitalism as a system based on exploitation.

Marx said his aim was to bring scientific method to political economy and in this way "reveal the law of motion of modern society". By showing how capitalist development was the precursor of a new, socialist mode of production, he aimed to provide a scientific foundation for the modern labour movement.

Capitalism has had a pretty good run now for about a hundred and fifty years. It's been tried and tested and what does the report card look like? Not bad, you say? Look at the goods we've produced for the welfare of the whole population.

Well, let's look at it. What you see depends on where you're standing. If you're in the belly of the beast, enjoying the fruits of stolen labor-power, it might look pretty good. But if you're one of the masses, a member of the working class struggling to keep body and soul together, one who has offered up the surplus value of your labor for your employer's profit, you might take a different view of the situation.

When you look around and see what capitalism has done to the earth and to the environment, it disgusts you further. Capitalist entrepreneurs have not only stolen part of your labor, but they've stolen the gifts of nature! The oil of the earth, the trees of the forest, the minerals and wealth of the mines. These are not man made objects for sale or profit. They should belong to no person or entity because they belong to everyone who walks the earth, like the air they breathe and the water that supports life. (The capitalists are trying to get a corner on that, too) At the same time, while they despoil the earth with their industrial operations, they try to hand off their mess as social cost to the community as a whole.

Chief Joseph, a leader of the Nez Perce tribe in the Pacific Northwest, once said, "I think of the Earth as our Mother."

I know what you're going to say, "The Soviet Union, a supposedly socialist nation made an even bigger mess of it." Yes, they did, and so is China, now. But the key word there is "supposedly". The Soviet Union was co-opted by a dictator, Stalin, after Lenin died and Trotsky was "axed" in 1940. Socialism is still being tested in various forms, in Scandinavia, in Cuba, now in South America. Hugo Chavez in Venezuela is bringing the nation closer to what socialism is supposed to look like. Like the geologic plates in the earth, economic systems move very slowly. They only change at times of sheer necessity, when they no longer serve the masses. That's why revolutions are so hard to come by.

"All roads lead to socialism," said Marx. What's wrong with looking for a better road?

As for the Havana cigar mentioned earlier, that's to puff on while taking this lesson in political economy. Or, as Rudyard Kipling might have said, "A lesson is only a lesson, but a good cigar is a smoke."

Conspiracy Theory

All that glitters is not gold and all that we think we see may not be what it seems to be.

Wikipedia, the internet encyclopedia, describes a conspiracy theory as: "attributing the ultimate cause of an event or chain of events ... to a secret, and often deceptive, plot by a covert alliance of powerful or influential people or organizations."

We know that the Bush family and the royal family of Saudi Arabia are close. We know that the bin Laden family, including maverick son, Osama, and the Saudi Arabia royal family are close. We know that of the nineteen 9/11 highjackers, most were Saudi Arabian. We know there is credible evidence of controlled demolition in the destruction of the World Trade Center towers. Devise your own conspiracy theory. The official one doesn't hold water.

In 2000, the President of the United States was appointed by the Supreme Court. In 2004, John Kerry, Democrat, received a plurality of the popular vote but lost the election by a few electoral votes.

How did this happen?

About three million absentee ballots were "lost". The Pentagon had shut down a website used to file overseas registrations. A consulting firm, hired by the Republican National Committee to register voters, was discovered shredding Democratic registrations. In several states, faulty electronic voting machines that left no paper trail, "spoiled" one million ballots, according to a federal commission. In Ohio, a pivotal state in the election, officials purged tens of thousands of eligible voters, neglected to process registration cards generated by Democratic voter drives and illegally derailed a recount that could have given Kerry the presidency.

"I've become convinced that the president's party mounted a massive, coordinated campaign to subvert the will of the people in 2004, "said

Robert F. Kennedy, Jr. "Across the country, Republican election officials and party stalwarts employed a wide range of illegal and unethical tactics to fix the election."

Was this a "conspiracy" to deprive John Kerry of victory and keep George W. Bush in office? Devise your own theory.

Remember The Iran-Contra Affair—popularly known as Iran Contra? Would you call it a conspiracy? You bet! It involved members of the Reagan Administration selling arms to Iran in the 1980s, so it could use the proceeds to fund the "Contras", a free-lance, anti-communist guerrilla organization out to get the Sandinista government in Nicaragua. This was done to circumvent an act of Congress, the Boland Amendment, which specifically made funding of the Contras by the US government illegal.

With George W. Bush, presently preparing a war against Iran, it's a bit ironic that 21 years ago, the Reagan administration (that included Vice-President George Bush, the elder) worked very hard to <u>sell</u> arms to the same Islamic revolutionary fundamentalists they're now planning to bomb.

The trio of bandoleros, credited for cooking up this scheme, were former Reagan National Security Advisors Robert McFarlane, John Poindexter and conspirator-at-large Col. Oliver North. In February 1986, 1000 TOW missiles, very handy for shooting down planes, were shipped to Iran. From May to November 1986, there were additional shipments of miscellaneous weapons and parts. The icing on the cake was just that; on a trip to Iran during the Iran-Contra affair, North and Robert McFarlane brought a bible and a chocolate cake (shaped like a key to symbolize the opening of improved relations) as gifts to the Ayatollah Khomeini to thank him for his arms purchases. Need we look for a conspiracy theory here?

The daddy of them all—Watergate. That one, conspiracy plus, shook the world for more than ten days. As we all remember or learned from history, it started with a third-rate burglary. Some plumbers from the Nixon White House (they fix leaks) broke into the Democratic Party Headquarters in the Watergate building in Washington in 1972, before the presidential elections, and planted some bugs. The bugs didn't work so they had to go back to find out what the problem was. That's when they got caught, exposing the White House dirty tricks squad, an enemies list, a secret campaign slush fund for the re-election of the president—and a cover-up that went with it. Of course it ended with the resignation of Nixon on August 9, 1974, before Congress could get around to impeaching him.

The mass media, particularly the Washington Post, gained new stature in exposing the conspiracy. The fourth estate redeemed its dignity. The work of reporters Bob Woodward and Carl Bernstein, in bringing the Watergate conspiracy to light, emboldened a new generation of journalists and gave a shot in the arm to the lost art of investigative reporting. Where are these reporters, now that we really need them! Yes, we have Seymour Hersh and *The New Yorker Magazine*. The Bush Administration needs to be "watergated"! Hirsh is doing his best. But the story hasn't penetrated.

Why are people so willing to delude themselves? I suppose it's part of human nature to lie to oneself or accept a lie put upon us rather than live with a truth too dark and painful to bear. Go with the flow. Internalize the conventional wisdom (which is too often wrong). But survival depends on truth.

We're at a point where we must decide to face reality or live in this fantasy world, constructed for us by a tissue of lies. A lying government is at the root of our problem. With global warming threatening the very existence of our plant, a catastrophic war in Iraq which we have already lost, with another one looming to distract our attention from the first, we need a very loud wake-up call.

Face the fact that the terrorists are us and the regime change we need is ours.

Self-Fulfilling Prophecies

A self-fulfilling prophecy—as defined by Robert K. Merton, 20th Century sociologist who coined the phrase—is that a prediction, in being made, actually causes itself to become true. There are a couple of vivid examples in the works right now.

In the nearly five years since 9/11 and the destruction of the World Trade Center in New York City, up to the alleged recently thwarted plot to destroy twelve commercial airliners in mid-flight between Great Britain and the United States, President Bush has been working furiously to bring about a self-fulfilling prophecy with his war on terror.

"War on Terror." The phrase is meaningless. What is terror? An emotion. You can't go to war against an emotion. But it's being used and promoted by the administration for its fear-producing effect and by the mainstream media as a rating or readership enhancer.

When the al-Qaeda 9/11 attack took place, instead of coordinating a massive international police action to apprehend Osama bin Laden, the brains of the operation, the United States, instead, decided to wipe out an independent country, Afghanistan. The justification was that Bin Laden had been given sanctuary there and was using the place for a terrorist training ground. Bush made it perfectly clear. He wanted Bin Laden "dead or alive" like a good Western lawman should. After some shock and awe bombing, the US Army's Special Forces hit the ground running, but flubbed an attempt to capture Bin Laden in the Tora Bora Mountains.

The Taliban, the regime in power, once courted by American oil companies and US government officials for concessions in the building of an oil pipeline across their country, was now demonized and driven out of power. The US has been carrying on a military operation against the Taliban's guerrilla force ever since and Afghanistan continues to be a terrorist producing machine.

The failures in Afghanistan did not deter George Bush's war on terror. He simply moved on to Iraq where he and his neo-con toadies, hiding under a rock in the Pentagon, always wanted to be. The self-fulfilling prophecy was picking up steam. Regime change was achieved in short order. Saddam Hussein was history within the first few weeks after the US Air Force's shock and awe bombing of Bagdad. But three and a half years later, the US military is still spinning its wheels in Iraq, bogged down in a quagmire, an occupation, an insurgency and a civil war all brewing at the same time. With more than 2,600 American servicemen dead, 20,000 wounded and $307 billion dollars (and counting) of American taxpayer treasure down the drain, Iraq is now a bigger and better terrorist producing operation than Afghanistan ever was. Isn't that punishing yourself? Isn't the war on terror creating Bush's very own self-fulfilling prophecy?

Two down, another to go. Lebanon. Bush wanted Hezbollah destroyed as much as Israel did. It was simple. Delay a cease fire in the UN and let Israel do the job. First stage in our thrust against Iran. So was Bush using Israel, or was Israel, the tail, wagging the dog? Israel and the United States have a "special relationship", an oft repeated truism. But do they always have the same national interests?

Yes, Iran has been sending rockets and missiles to Hezbollah for its war against Israel. It's been deplored around the block. The United States has been sending Black Hawk helicopters and bunker-busting bombs to Israel for its war against Hezbollah. I haven't heard a word whispered about it. Is there a double standard here?

Israel's great fear—it will be pushed into the sea. It's a great fear, and it's understandable. It's been there since 1948, since the Israeli-Palestinian question has failed to be resolved.

I'm old enough to remember the great upsurge of feeling when the United Nations established the State of Israel in 1948. A people torn from the Holocaust, returning to an ancestral land. It was inspiring. It might have been a good idea once, a Zionist movement led mostly by Ashkenazi Jews from Northern and Central Europe. They brought with them a great deal of knowledge and a great deal of know-how. They promised to, and they did, make the desert bloom, and Jews, everywhere, rejoiced at the bounty they would bring to the region. But then, what happened? Did they extend the hand of friendship to their Arab neighbors? Was it spurned? Could they create an atmosphere of mutual cooperation and trust between the two strains of Semitic peoples? Apparently not. The country was born in violence, with the expulsion of thousands of Palestinians, and the Israelis have had to defend themselves ever since. They've built a mighty military force (which we've just seen in action). Could they eliminate the Hezbollah with this enormous power? Apparently not.

Are people in such denial that they learn nothing from history, or even from events of the recent past. Look at Iraq. Look at Vietnam. Look at Algeria. Look at Tito of Yugoslavia or France under Nazi occupation during World War II. As the Vietcong used to say, "we live among the people like fish in water."

So is Israeli, too, working mightily to achieve the thing it dreads the most, a "self-fulfilling prophecy?"

Skirting the R-Word

The US economy is walking a tight-rope.

The sharp drop-off in growth in the first quarter of 2007, and the expected weak second and third quarters of less than 2% growth, caused the widely watched UCLA Anderson Forecast, a leading national economic forecaster, to conclude that although we may not actually be in a recession "it is certainly close."

Only days later, the New York Times reported a $3.2 billion move by Bear Stearns, the investment bank, to bail out one of its hedge funds that was collapsing because of bad debts on sub-prime mortgages.

The Anderson Forecast saw the slowed economy as lasting longer than previously expected. Weakness in the housing market and higher gasoline prices are starting to affect consumer spending. California, hit by a "double-whammy" from construction and mortgage finance, foreshadows a drag on the rest of the economy.

A recession is usually defined as a decline in a country's real Gross Domestic Product (GDP) for two or more successive quarters.

Market-oriented, or capitalist, economies are characterized by economic cycles. The business cycle represents swings between periods of relatively rapid growth and periods of relative stagnation. Capitalism is noted for its cycles. Its nature is to boom and bust.

There have been a number of such bounces—recessions, financial crises, depressions and just plain downturns since the Panic of 1819, the first major financial crisis in the United States, when our capitalist system was still in diapers. That one lasted until 1824 before the economy recovered only to be hit again by the Panic of 1837 which lasted until 1843, due to bank failures and the public's lack of confidence in paper money. It was followed by the Panic of 1857 and the Panic of 1873 prompted by the failure of Jay Cooke & Co., the largest bank in the United States at the time. This panic finally burst the post-Civil War speculative bubble.

Wars are frequently associated with these cycles because wars are used to stimulate the economy enough to help pull it out of the slump. The so-called "Long Depression" that began with the Panic of 1873 lasted until 1896 and spread throughout the world.

President William McKinley, who took office in 1897, called himself "an advance agent of prosperity" and his administration wowed the robber barons with his dramatic action. One of his first acts was to convince Congress to annex Hawaii and make it a US Territory. Something new had been added to the US form of government, and McKinley said this about it: "We need Hawaii just as much as we did California."

McKinley found another way of enhancing prosperity. The explosion (cause unknown) on the USS Maine in Havana harbor killing 274 men, gave him a reason to declare war on Spain in 1898.

Victory in the Spanish-America War after only 109 days, garnered for the United States ownership of former Spanish colonies—Puerto Rico, the Philippines and Guam. Secretary of State John Hay called it a "splendid little war!" We also took control of Cuba, expelling the Spanish and ending the insurrection there. The naval war in Cuba and the Philippines was the most profitable war in US history. The United States was well on its way to becoming a first rate imperial power.

Then along came the Panic of 1907; a run on Knickerbocker Trust Company stock that set the stage for future economic problems.

After the post-WWI recession that caused severe hyperinflation in Europe, production in North America took a dive.

The Great Depression hit with a crash. First, the stock market in 1929; then the banking collapse that sparked a global downturn.

Despite Roosevelt's gallant effort with the NRA and other supportive devices like the TVA and the WPA, the economy stumbled along well into the beginning of World War II. The economy saved by another war.

Recession came again after the Korean War in 1953. They just won't quit. We used the Vietnam War to get away from that one. But it only bogged us down until 1975 when we lost to the Vietnamese communists.

Before the war ended, we had the 1973 oil crisis—a quadrupling of oil prices by OPEC and high government spending—a war and stagflation at the same time.

In 1979, the Iranian Revolution was a bolt from the blue. Not only did the Ayatollahs seize American hostages but they also skyrocketed the price of oil. The result: early 1980s recession and drop in commodity prices that lasted until the year 2000.

From 1988 to 1992 we saw the collapse of junk bonds and a stock market crash that led to a recession in much of the world.

The Japanese recession started in 1991 and is still going on. The collapse of a real estate bubble and more fundamental problems halted Japan's once astronomical growth. The general Asian financial crisis started in 1997. The collapse of the Thai currency inflicted damage on many of the Asian economies.

An early 2000 recession, the collapse of the Dot Com Bubble, the 9/11 attack, the Afghanistan and Iraq Wars are now contributing to our present problems.

George W. Bush seems to be a spiritual follower of President McKinley. The cost of the Iraq war will wind up costing American taxpayers an estimated 1 trillion dollars. Can you wrap your head around that figure? In numbers it looks like this: $1,000,000,000,000. Or, if you want to look at it another way; $200 million a day or $3 billion a week, by Congressional estimates.

Think of what can be done, in this country, with that kind of money—rebuilding the infrastructure, our schools and our hospitals, paying for National Health Insurance, clean air and fresh water and development of pollution free energy, and that's only for starters.

Lawrence Lindsey, economic adviser in the Bush Administration, when asked by The Wall Street Journal about the cost of the Iraq war replied:

"The successful prosecution of the war would be good for the economy."

The Road Not Taken

James Lovelock, a British scientist with a worldwide reputation as a leader in environmental awareness, has recently declared that the world has already passed the point of no return. Civilization, as we know it, is unlikely to survive.

When and where did humanity miss that fork in the road, the turn that might have led to a better place than we are in, today? Was it, as Robert Frost conjectured in his poem "The Road Not Taken", "the one less traveled by?"

Dr. Lovelock is the author of a book and a theory called "Gaia" that considers the planet Earth as a self-regulated living being which has, up until now, been capable of healing itself from environment damage—but no more. The Earth can no longer recover from the greenhouse effect causing the global warming that is well under way.

Although the scientific community may deem this to be conventional wisdom, the general public seems to be in a state of denial—too frightened—or perhaps, too confused to face the facts.

Where did we go wrong? Was it after World War II, or after World War I, or maybe the Cold War? Everybody knows how destructive war can be to the environment. The turning point may have occurred as far back as England's Industrial Revolution in the 18th Century. Who can count the number of wars since then?

But why speculate, since there's no way out. No turning back. As Robert Frost says,

"… knowing how way leads on to way,
I doubt if I shall ever come back."

Some might say that where the two roads diverged goes back to the Roman Empire when the Romans invaded Europe and divided all Gaul into three parts.

Or it might even go back to the great civilizations of the Middle East, Mesopotamia, for instance, the cradle of civilization, where Iraq is today—where the Arabs invented numerals including the number "zero", a major contribution to the world's culture. Could this have led to the current crisis? As one wag put it, "try doing long division using Roman numerals".

Then again, there was the invention of gunpowder by the Chinese, but for about ten centuries they only used it for fireworks. There couldn't have been much harm created there.

To get to one possible fork in the road, I think we have to go back to the Enclosure Acts in Britain, where they drove the farmers off the land so that budding venture capitalists could enclose it for raising sheep to supply the wool that fed the looms that the Industrial Revolution built. Bingo! There was *profit!*

And as Robert Frost says, "… knowing how way leads on to way", let's follow the path of the profit system.…

Adam Smith (1723–1790), a Scottish moral philosopher and the first political economist, was right there on the scene when it all happened—and he gave it a name—Capitalism. And in his book, "The Wealth of Nations", Adam Smith told us that a free market system would be like an "invisible hand" that would guide capitalism to stability and prosperity. There are some American capitalists who still believe that, or say they do.

The Capitalist Road has led us to a need for constantly expanding production or face depression. In other words, grow or die.

For a planet, gasping for breath, the need is quite the opposite—restrict industrial growth—or die! Production for profit and environmental conservation are conflicting forces that cannot be reconciled. Well, I guess we've got to go back to the drawing board on that.

Maybe that road diverged at the time of "primitive communism" when there were no social classes, no private property and no state. We lived in small groups in an agricultural society, working together for the common good, where the slogan would have been, "To each according to his need, from each according to his ability."

Maybe working together for the common good can still happen. By adopting that slogan and enforcing it's necessary imperatives we can still make a glorious new world of global democracy. That's what Robert Frost would have said. When he came to those divergent roads he wanted to travel both:

> "And looked down one as far as I could
>> To where it bent in the undergrowth;
>> Then took the other, as just as fair,
>> And having perhaps the better claim,
>> Because it was grassy and wanted wear;"

And here's where Frost gets a little ambivalent … which road do we go with?

>> "Though as for that the passing there
>> Had worn them really about the same."

Yeah, well, now he tells us …

>> "I shall be telling this with a sigh
>> Somewhere ages and ages hence:
>> Two roads diverged in a wood, and I—
>> I took the one less traveled by,
>> And that has made all the difference.

The whole poem, below:

Robert Frost: The Road Not Taken (1915)

> Two roads diverged in a yellow wood,
> And sorry I could not travel both
> And be one traveler, long I stood
> And looked down one as far as I could
> To where it bent in the undergrowth.

Then took the other, as just as fair,
And having perhaps the better claim,
Because it was grassy and wanted wear;
Though as for that the passing there
Had worn them really about the same.

And both that morning equally lay
In leaves no step had trodden black.
Oh, I kept the first for another day!
Yet knowing how way leads on to way,
I doubted if I should ever come back.

I shall be telling this with a sigh
Somewhere ages and ages hence:
Two roads diverged in a wood, and I—
I took the one less traveled by,
And that has made all the difference.

Hillary and Bill—the Bonnie and Clyde of Politics

"We rob banks!" said Clyde Barrow.

"We rob you of your political initiative …" Hillary Clinton might have said when she and her husband, the President of the United States, managed to kill the chances for Universal Health Care for all Americans by, deliberately or otherwise, playing into the hands of the Insurance Industry and their HMO backers. They set the movement for a single payer plan back a generation.

Hillary Rodham Clinton is now the Democratic front-runner in the race for the Presidency of the United States in 2008. We are currently in that murky, foggy area where the runners are cantering before they break out in the open field gallop to the finish line.

Bill Clinton may not have robbed banks, but he robbed gay and lesbian citizens of their civil rights with his "Don't Ask, Don't Tell" policy for the armed forces:

"Sexual orientation will not be a bar to service unless manifested by homosexual conduct…., or a marriage or attempted marriage to someone of the same gender."—quoted in "The Pentagon's New Policy Guidelines on Homosexuals in the Military."

The policy has continued under the Bush Administration, unofficially, stretched to include gays and lesbians in the general population when it ran up against issues of gay marriage.

Before the end of his second term, Clinton was fighting impeachment in the House and the threat of being ousted by the Senate charged with perjury—lying about his relationship with Monica Lewinsky. His Secretary of State, Madeleine Albright, was urging him to wag the dog. That bit of advice came in handy. How else do you rob your constituents of their political initiative? Start a war. We know from historical experience that it works every time.

While the representatives in the US Congress were shouting "Ethnic Cleansing"—Bill was getting his bombers ready. The issue somehow got mixed up with the Holocaust and genocide. The mainstream media picked up the chant and CNN led the charge with woman warrior, Christiane Amanpour, the Amazon of the network, married to Mme Albright's pet assistant, James Rubin (conflict of interest?) when she covered the exodus from Kosovo.

So we bombed a country back to the Stone Age. It was only Serbia. Maybe its leader, Slobodan Milošević, deserved it. But the Serbian people didn't.

The Democratic Party has always been known as the party of the big tent, room for everybody—let many flowers bloom—left-labor-progressives, blacks, other minorities, immigrants, radicals, students and even conservationists.

In the 1996 Presidential election, the Barrow gang, I mean the Clinton gang brought in their big gun to advise the campaign—Dick Morris—the Karl Rove of his time.

"Don't worry about those losers on the left," Dick Morris must have told his pal, Bill, "they're only your base. They have nowhere to go. You'll get their votes. It's those weak-kneed Republican compassionate conservatives, on the right, you have to go after."

And Dick knew what he was talking about. Move to the right and call it the center. The Democratic Leadership Council was formed and they eased in on the Republicans and captured a big enough chunk of their votes to win the election.

Our two-party system became one party with two faces—neither of them very pretty. Whatever happened to the "loyal opposition"? It was nowhere to be found. Where have all the flowers gone? The tent must have collapsed on them.

So we now have an "oligarchy"—dictionary definition: from the Greek for "rule of the few"—this is a form of government in which power is centralized in the hands of an organized elite. Their power is maintained by shaping the law to restrict the people and remove any need to consult them or be accountable to them. Sounds like America to me. The Clinton strategy paved the way for the Bush Administration to come.

"We rob banks!" said Clyde Barrow, "not people."

Where are you Dick Morris, now that Hillary really needs you? Getting ready for that triangulation-strangulation strategy you used so successfully for Bill in the 1990s?

The strategy of lesser-evilism is alive and well in the 21st Century.

In March of 2003, right after the lawless invasion of Iraq, that Hillary and other Democrats voted to authorize, Dan Rather, still anchor of the CBS Evening News, interviewed his Commander-in-Chief.

"We're at war," said George W. Bush.

"Yes Sir," said Dan Rather to his President and Commander-in-Chief, "Where do you want me to stand? How high do you want me to jump? Sir, Yes Sir"

Where were you when independent journalism died?

Fascism Unmasked

Defining Fascism is a little like describing an elephant in the dark. It depends on what part of the animal you're touching. If you're holding the trunk, you can say it's a fat snake. If you're holding the tail you can say it's a whip.

There's a rancid smell of fascism in the air lately and nobody is doing anything about it: like the apathy of the German people before the Reichstag fire in 1933. Political scientist, Dr. Lawrence W. Britt, published the results of his study of Fascism in Free Inquiry Magazine defining 14 of its characteristics, but he, too, describes the symptoms, not the cause.

Let's go to the source—Benito Mussolini, strongman of Italy before World War II, who instituted Fascism and coined the word.

Mussolini defined Fascism as Corporatism. When corporations take over government by whatever means, by buying up politicians or getting their hands on the wheels of power, they are merging corporate power and government—that's Fascism. All the other depredations of democracy follow.

It's a dictatorship; it's a loss of freedom; it's condoning torture: it's controlling mass media; it's fraudulent elections. It can be all of those things.

Sound familiar? Where did Habeas Corpus go? Who's violating the Geneva Conventions? Who's surveilling American citizens without warrants? What is Guantanamo Bay? A concentration camp? Harboring enemy combatants at the moment, but being prepared for naughty, dissident American citizens one day, maybe?

In a democracy, officials of government who do these kinds of things are committing high crimes and misdemeanors. Impeachment is the constitutional weapon used to defend the Republic and remove those found guilty in the court of Congress. Our President and our Vice-President are both impeachable, according to these rules. So, what's happening?

Well, some people are saying, Bush and Cheney's terms end in 2009. Is it worth all the discombobulation if they're going to be out in a year and a half? You're damned right it is! People have to be accountable for their crimes!

Yet, our Democratic Speaker of the House, Nancy Pelosi, says "impeachment is off the table". Democratic members of the Senate and the House fuss and fume about the Iraq War while holding the purse in their hands. They have the power and the constitutional right to cut off funding for the war. But what do they do? They give Bush the money he wants to go on killing Americans and Iraqis. What is the war about? Corporate profits.

We all know what has to be done to end this shameful process.

Campaign finance reform is not good enough. We need campaign finance revolution. All campaign costs, for all candidates for all offices, are determined and paid for by the people—through their government. It would cost a lot less than a war. Make it a crime to show money to a candidate who is running for office.

Fat chance! That's like asking politicians to vote themselves out of a job. They bought that spot with the campaign money that they raised and they think they own the seat. (Yes, in cahoots with their donors, the corporate, monied class.) We have to get them out. And we can do it.

Make every American citizen a voter. It's a matter of education, as it always is. Educate and Organize. It's going to be a tough job here because five or six corporate conglomerates control the mass media and just about everything we see, hear and read. And they're always trying to tell us how to think.

We don't have a democracy in this country. We have an oligarchy and it's getting tighter. Nothing new about that. It goes back to ancient Greece. It derived from the Greek word, "Oligarkhia",(a contraction of "few" and "rule") a form of government where political power is in the hands of a small, elite segment of society, distinguished by wealth, family and military power. Karl Marx added to that list: "owners of the means of production". As they gain increasing control over government, we get closer to Benito Mussolini's definition of "Corporatism".

We're looking fascism right in the face. Let's go back to some of the symptoms described by Dr. Britt, who studied the fascist regimes of Hitler's Germany, Mussolini's Italy, Franco's Spain, Suharto's Indonesia and several Latin countries, and noted what they all had in common.

Dr. Britt found a powerful and continuous drive toward nationalism in Fascist regimes. They exploit patriotic mottos, slogans and symbols. Flags are seen everywhere, even on clothing and in public displays. (Do you wear a flag pin in your lapel to prove your patriotism?)

Create fear. The War on Terror. (A total anomaly) Terror is an emotion, not an enemy combatant. Fear of enemies, and the need for security, breeds the feeling that it's okay to ignore the violation of human rights and give up a few of your own civil rights to attain it.

Dr. Britt points out that because the organizing power of labor is the only real threat to a Fascist government, labor unions are either eliminated entirely or severely suppressed. (Look at the sorry state of our once powerful labor movement. Where is John L. Lewis now that we really need him?)

These are a few of Dr. Britt's 14 points. Take them seriously. Don't temporize. Organize!

Some people say we're on the ragged edge of fascism. Some people say it's already here. On a scale of one to ten, where do you think we stand?

Can We Kill the Beast?

During World War II, around the time of the Battle of Stalingrad (considered the bloodiest battle in human history) the Russians had a toast.

They'd drink "To the Breaking of the Back of the Fascist Beast!"

The ritual caught on, and even in the west, many of us raised our glasses to it.

The Russians eventually succeeded in their drive, and the free world rejoiced, when on February 2, 1943, a good chunk of Hitler's Nazi Army became toast. In the Battle of Stalingrad, the Wehrmacht lost their 6th Army and 4th Panzer Army, totaling about 850,000 men. Russian casualties were around 1.2 million, civilian and military. The joke going around then was, "at that rate, pretty soon, no more Germans".

The Allies dragged their feet until D-Day, June 6, 1944, before opening a second front at Normandy. The Allies finally had to do it as the Red Army came storming back across the continent, continuing to wipe out even bigger chunks of the Wehrmacht. After that, it was a race to Berlin.

I am reminded of the toast—because a "Fascist Beast" is looking right into our face, at this very moment.

"What is Fascism?" you might ask. And as former President Bill Clinton might have answered, "it depends what the meaning of "fascism" is?

Well, let's go right to the source: Italian dictator Benito Mussolini, a former member of the Axis, defined it this way: "Fascism should more appropriately be called Corporatism because it is a merger between state and corporate power".

That sounds a lot like America to me. Fascism creeps in on little cats' feet.

The word "Fascist" or "Fascism" is derived from the "Fasces", an icon representing the strength and power of Ancient Rome—a cylindrical bundle of elm or birch rods bound together by red bands, from which an ax-head protrudes. Mussolini managed to bring the symbol into the modern world to depict his own power over the contemporary Italian nation.

Unless we reverse course on two fronts—Iraq and erosion of Constitutional rights—we'll be sliding down that slippery slope.

Wars, today, are not the kind we're good at—pitched battles with heavy armor and lots of men and B-2 bombers. We are allowing the arms merchants to determine the kinds of weapons we use. They, of course, are selling the taxpayers the weapons on which they make the most money. Those in the Pentagon, making the decisions, are in revolving doors, going from arms merchant to government arms procurer in one circular movement, one example of blurring the distinctions between "corporate power and the state".

Since we hadn't learned our lesson in Vietnam, we are suffering the same punishment in Iraq, today—more than 2,100 of our precious young men and women uselessly killed, more than 15,000 brutally wounded. And more than 227 billion dollars, and counting, of our treasure gone.

Abram tanks, Humvees and Bradley fighting vehicles are pitched against IEDs (improvised explosive devices) and suicide bombers. These simple devices work fine for the insurgents fighting the occupation forces where the insurgents have the support of a sizable portion of the population.

Elections and purple fingers notwithstanding, the people know that such shenanigans under the watchful eye of American occupation forces will get them nowhere.

President Bush assures the American people, over and over again, that he will protect them against terror. Yet, he has created the two greatest terror mills in history—Iraq and Afghanistan. If he keeps this up, he'll get the award for the most unintended consequences.

The good news is: Congress seems to be growing some spine. Some Republicans, finally, may be standing up for their conservative principles.

Except for the courageous stand of John Murtha, Congressman from Pennsylvania's 12th Congressional District, most Democrats seem to be locked into the positions they imposed upon themselves by their original support for Bush's war. Unless they change, and move back to their base, which used to be their mainstay, under the big tent, the left, liberal, working class, small business, poor, minority, black, Hispanic, gay and lesbian, and, oh yes, women and youth constituency, they will continue to be dead men walking. Democrats must abjure being led, again, down the Dick Morris garden path of Hillary and Bill's triangulation-strangulation strategy, still being trodden by the Democratic so-called Leadership Council.

Now they have the opportunity to seize the initiative—call for the immediate withdrawal of troops from Iraq and stop the unlawful surveillance of American citizens by our own spy agencies, which President George W. Bush just admitted having ordered. Did you ever hear of a sitting President confess to breaking the law? The outburst of anger is growing across the country and Bush is acting like a punch-drunk fighter on the ropes.

If the nascent anti-war movement can rally itself by March of 2006, the third anniversary of the war, they might be able to deliver the final punch and save America from sliding further down the slippery slope.

The Eagles, in *Hotel California,* put it this way:

And in the master's chambers,
They gathered for the feast,
They stab it with their steely knives,
But they just can' kill the beast.

Let's stop the encroaching Beast in its tracks, so there will be no need to drink to the breaking of its back.

Salud! Na sdrovia!

Winners and Losers

There are winners and losers, an old, bearded, 19th Century economist told us once. That's the way the system works.

Capitalists have been chewing each other up since the Industrial Revolution, said Karl Marx, world famous analyst of "the system", and the battle of mergers and acquisitions still goes on. Dog eat dog. There are always a few good men left at the table; but winners grow increasingly fewer and richer. There are now 946 billionaires in the world, according to Forbes, and 371 of them are in the United States with Bill Gates and Warren Buffett topping the list with $56 billion and $52 billion respectively. So, we wind up with a few winners, a lot of losers, and a plethora of monopolies and oligopolies.

You can see it everywhere in our economy, today. In the main stream media, five or six oligopolies control just about everything we read, see, hear and think. Multi-national corporations own most of the means of production, distribution and retail trade. The concentration of capital displaced the handworker and the crafts-worker. Hitching the computer to the assembly line, called cybernation, has further exploded production. Independent producers have been eliminated by cybernetic competition. Mom and Pop operations have gotten lost in the shuffle.

Capitalism reverses the law of gravity, with money flowing up instead of down. As the rich become richer, the poor have children. With the explosion in technology, productivity of labor is going through the roof. But the purchasing power of the laborer is falling through the floor. We can't keep that up for long. When workers can't afford to buy the things they make and their jobs are siphoned out of the country "with a giant sucking sound" as one former sage put it, the economy goes flatter than a bad soufflé. The last time it happened we had a sudden deflation and a persistent depression we could barely crawl out of even with the stimulus of World War II.

Our economic system is under stress, again. We can't seem to keep it afloat without massive production of military hardware. That could be one reason George Bush tries to keep us in a state of perpetual war. Our military budget has reached $532 billion for 2007; with another half trillion for the cost of the Afghanistan and Iraq War. (Not to mention the human costs.) Why? It isn't producing better schools or improving infrastructure or providing social services for the people who need it in this country. The Bush Administration claims to be exporting democracy while killing it here.

The Rovian brainchild, the "war on terror", was devised to keep us shadow-boxing with fear. Even though that concept is finally running out of steam, there is no "loyal opposition" in this country to drive a stake through its heart. (Where is a vampiric Democratic Party, now that we really need one?)

Let's get back to basics. Why is Marxist economics never, or almost never, mentioned in polite society or discussed in the mainstream media? *Absolut Verboten!* You won't be brainwashed into becoming an ideologue if you examine it, but you might get an idea or two that makes sense to you.

One of the reasons for our backwardness may be explained by the failure of our labor movement (when we had one) to become politicized. The closest we came to it was the emergence of John L. Lewis and the organization of the CIO (Congress of Industrial Organizations) and the sit-down strikes of 1936 and 1937. Still, the orientation of the labor movement was stuck in economic issues, (hours, wages, benefits) and they left the politics to the Democratic Party where they thought they had a front row seat under the big tent. Too bad. Seats are easy to lose, as the workers of America found out.

We never had a real political Labor Party in this country, fighting for the rights of labor, minorities and the common people, as there are in many of the other industrialized democracies in the world. Several attempts were made in earlier days; the Farmer Labor Party and the Progressive Party in the time of Robert La Follette and Gene Debs. But they never got off the ground. The country was too new. It was too full of rugged individualists and a few robber barons.

Still, Capitalism had its day. It promoted the greatest economic development in human history; the upper, middle and skilled working class enjoyed most of its benefits, still a minority of the population. It left masses of people out in the cold.

So where is the class struggle? Don't look, it's there. We're not talking about social classes now. Just for the hell of it, let's call them the proletariat and the bourgeoisie. Oh, so you don't think they exist …? Well, now …

Are you a member of the proletariat and earn your livelihood by selling your labor power and being paid a wage or salary for your labor time? Or are you a member of the bourgeoisie and get your income, not from your labor, but from the labor appropriated from the workers who created the wealth in the form of surplus value? The income of capitalists, in the form of profits, is based on their exploitation of the workers. And that's a fact.

Not all class struggle is violent or necessarily radical. The strike is the classic form of class struggle by workers in a union. It may also be expressed on a larger scale by support of political causes and the fight for a Labor Party. Some form of Socialist government may be its ultimate goal.

On the employers' side, union-busting and lobbying for anti-union laws are their main forms of carrying on the class struggle. Not all class struggle is a threat to capitalism—or even to the authority of an individual capitalist.

You want a revolution? Well, first, you're going to have to let Capitalism dig its own grave. A little understood thesis of Marx is that Socialist revolution doesn't come from the outside. It only happens when the system in power can no longer fulfill the needs of the masses. It's in the process of digging the hole now.

We may not have too long to wait.

Let's Hear it for Chuck!

Chuck Hagel, conservative Republican Senator from Nebraska, and potential candidate for President in 2008, may shape up to be the real thing.

In an interview with Wil S. Hylton of GQ magazine, Hagel said this about the Iraq war: "I am not willing to sacrifice more young men and women for a policy that isn't working ... billions of dollars going into this hole. It will erode our standing in the Middle East and the world. It will destroy our force structure. It will divide this country in a bitter way not seen since Vietnam."

No mealy mouthed equivocation here, as we've been hearing from Democrats who have thrown their hats into the ring. But GQ's Mr. Hylton never asked Chuck Hagel the chippie question, "Do you want all US troops out of Iraq, now!"

I still don't know how he would answer that one. But, Hagel's pronouncements on the subject, thus far, are a lot better than anything I've heard from the front-running Democrats; Hillary Clinton (D) New York, who says anything Bush can do, she can do better, or Barack Obama (D) Illinois, who says, "combat forces should be out of Iraq by spring of 2008 to end 'a foreign policy disaster'.

If the Iraq war is "a foreign policy disaster" why wait until the spring of 2008 to get our troops out?

It seems that both parties are tied up in knots. They've heard the voice of the people, loud and clear in the 2006 mid-term elections in which the Democrats won both the House and the Senate and were expected to do something—to act in some decisive way. The vote was a direct and unequivocal repudiation of Bush and his war.

The people want out!

Can't their representatives in Congress get the message?

The trouble is, in this era, Congress is more the creature of Corporate America than it is the representative of the people. But that can change. There have been periods in our history when it has and it will surely happen again.

Conservative Republicans are beginning to break their ties to the Bush Administration and reclaim their heritage. Chuck Hagel's stand may be an indication of the political tectonic plates beginning to shift beneath the surface. Senator John Warner of Virginia may be another. War has a transforming effect on political parties. They realign themselves with time and the state of the people's clout.

Remember the Whig Party? It flourished during the era of Jacksonian democracy and operated from 1832 to 1856. Just before the Civil War, the Whig party was shattered by the defection of the Northern Whigs over the issue of slavery. The Whigs supported the supremacy of Congress over the Executive Branch and could boast of such members as Daniel Webster and Henry Clay. How long would George W. Bush last if he had to stand up against men of that character, today? They'd cut funding for Bush's war in a New York minute.

Impeachment would be on the table. From the very beginning, Congress jealously guarded its constitutional right to declare war and certainly wouldn't have given any president a blank check to go war. Abraham Lincoln was a Whig representative in the Illinois House of Representatives for four consecutive terms. When the Whig Party split, he left politics for a while but eventually came back as a Republican, was elected President and saved the union in the Civil War.

Can it be saved again? Considering where we've come from, a slave society in the 1860s, we've made some progress in a hundred and fifty years. We've had some strong democratic leadership during those years. For one, "Fighting Bob" La Follette (R) Senator from Wisconsin and a force behind the Progressive Party and the Farmer-Labor Party in the early 20th Century.

La Follette made some cogent remarks that are very applicable to today's political climate [sic] "The underlying reason why both parties have failed to take the people's side in the present crisis is that neither party can openly attack the real evils which are undermining representative government without convicting themselves of treachery to the voters during their recent tenure in office".

We also had the mighty Eugene V. Debs during that period, labor leader, Socialist, political activist, Presidential candidate who ran four times, the last from prison and got over a million votes. And then there was the journalist, John Reed who documented the Russian Revolution in his book "Ten Days That Shook the World.

And we had the great John L. Lewis who organized the coal miners and during the Great Depression, the CIO (Congress of Industrial Organizations), all part of the great American democratic tradition. More recently, Martin Luther King, Jr. and the Civil Rights Movement of the 1960s.

The people of this country are yearning for a leader, out of our great tradition, one who will tell them the truth and lead them out of both the domestic and foreign policy disasters that the Bush Administration has brought upon us.

Can you live up to that, Chuck Hagel?

That's a Good Idea, Bury It!

You know that this country is approaching the end of its political and economic senses when it buries good ideas and extols bad ones.

Everybody knows that the principle of insurance is a good idea. We all kick in to a great big pot. The broader the participation, the wider the coverage, the less the premium and the bigger the payout can be.

For health, why not make it the entire population? Everybody needs health care. Instead of the patchwork quilt of employer plans, HMOs and for-profit insurance companies that cherry pick, leave millions uninsured, breed inefficiency and high healthcare costs, why not let the government do it? It's called the single-payer plan. The government is the single payer. Out of taxes—everybody's covered. Cut out the bureaucratic boondoggle. The money goes where it's intended, not into the stock options of the CEO's of the big insurance companies. No profiteering on your health or mine.

Just about every first world industrial nation, except the United States, has single-payer—also called Universal Health Insurance—what the critics call "socialized medicine". Excuse me for using a taboo expression. The propaganda mill works overtime to make sure single-payer doesn't happen here. It's too good an idea; bury it! Of course, the insurance industry has a hand in keeping it buried. A big hand … and not an invisible one. And we let them get away with it.

Now, tax cuts…. that's a highly praised objective. Taxes are associated with death. Get rid of them. Everybody loves tax cuts. Who can not vote for a politician who favors tax cuts? Keep the money in your pocket; why give it to the government? Cut entitlements, Social Security, Medicare, etc. but increase discretionary spending, money appropriated by Congress for things like the military and foreign aid. The Iraq war is a good example. That's discretionary, up to about a trillion dollars worth, and counting.

We used to have a progressive tax system in this country. President Roosevelt called for "soaking the rich". During the Eisenhower administration, people in the highest income brackets paid the most taxes. At one time, the top tax bracket was about 90%. There was a more equitable distribution of wealth. Of course, the rich didn't like that, and through the years they whittled away at it until they got it down to 39.6%, and falling. Republican administrations have always proposed tax cuts for the rich. George W. Bush has come up with the biggest and wants to make it permanent. They cut inheritance taxes, pejoratively called "death" taxes, and they reduced capital gains taxes even further.

While wealth flows up, poverty flows down.

As Anatole France, late 19th Century French writer, once said, "The law, in its majestic equality, forbids the rich as well as the poor to sleep under bridges, to beg in the streets, and to steal their bread."

What about "deregulation"? We've heard a lot about that for many years. It's a nagging problem. Corporations are always fighting to be free of government regulation. Get that "invisible hand" waving, make free trade agreements and boost globalization. That, they say, is how they create jobs.

A good idea? Thomas Friedman, columnist for the *New York Times,* thinks so. The world is flat, he says. He likes to hear that sucking sound, Ross Perot described, of good jobs and manufacturing plants flying out of the country. We've seen the results. Runaway Capitalism.

With deregulation, the fleecing of the States by the energy companies has become routine, giving us the "Enron effect" and other corporate disasters.

Give them a free hand? You'll see corporate bounty hunting on the world as never before. Multi-national corporations trumping nations.

Never let a bad idea go unrewarded.

Unionization. Now that's a good idea. Bury it! The Labor Union movement in this country has just about been buried alive. They used to keep the economy in better balance by fighting for higher wages and better working conditions. Not much, any more. When was the last time you saw workers out on strike? Or heard that John Sweeney, president of the AFL-CIO, has done something. Back at the 2005 national convention?

The Reagan Revolution began the attack on labor in 1981 by crushing the air traffic controllers union, PATCO. The attrition has continued ever since.

Union organizing was made respectable in 1935 when, in the depth of the Great Depression, Roosevelt put through the National Labor Relations Act. The Act guaranteed the right of employees to organize and to bargain collectively. This may have been the first instance of making legal the right to strike for better wages and working conditions. The National Labor Relations Board (NLRB) was set up to help labor get its share of the pie. Labor's freedom to fight led to the famous sit down strikes of 1936 and '37 that brought General Motors to its knees and allowed the creation of the strongest unions this country had ever seen—the auto workers, the mine workers, the steel workers, among many industrial unions and brought forth men like John L. Lewis, the Reuther Brothers, Walter and Victor, labor leaders larger than life, who organized the new and powerful CIO that later merged with the AFL. It brought the United States worldwide respect and attention. Where has it all gone?

Union Organizing? It was a good idea. They buried it!

Today, the key word is competition. Our workers have to compete with the most underpaid workers of the world. Cooperate with industry, our workers are told, or else—your jobs are at stake! An old, old song. They might have to give up some of their profits, would be more like the truth.

It's a very short race to the bottom, but we haven't hit rock bottom yet. We can still dig up some of these buried ideas.

We forget how fast things can change—when it's time for them to change.

Werewolf of Washington

From under what rock did he emerge that made it necessary to drag him kicking and screaming out of two capitalist entities, the US Department of Defense and the World Bank?

Paul Dundes Wolfowitz is no run-of-the-mill political bureaucrat. He's a neo-con with teeth.

His last rampage of destruction at the World Bank, a supposedly goody-goody organization of banks, dispenses loans to third world countries thereby putting them into debt. This is nothing but an ingenious way of impoverishing them further, an imperialist tactic, making it easier to control their regimes and steal their resources.

The United States contributes most of the funds so they have most of the clout in running the Bank. Making Wolfowitz president of the World Bank Group was an example of that clout.

When he got the job, in 2005, he was criticized for keeping aid from reaching places where it was needed. He promised to fight government corruption, but charges of nepotism hanging over him gave Wolfowitz an aura of hypocrisy, and skepticism about his anti-corruption promises was widespread.

The way he ran the Bank, primarily with the interest of the United States in mind, raised the hackles of some of the other countries that had an interest in how the Bank dispensed its cash. Other capitalist nations wanted their fair share of the pie.

Wolfowitz shot himself in the foot when he promoted his girl friend, an employee at the World Bank, giving her a whopping raise. That must have been the last straw for a majority of participating banks; the wedge used to get him out.

After some pawing of the ground, backing and filling, a compromise was reached. Wolfowitz threw in the towel. Part of the deal, it seems, was that the United States will be able, again, to pick the replacement.

The World Bank, apparently, is the place where discredited US Secretaries of Defense go to die. Robert McNamara, the former Secretary of Defense in the Lyndon Johnson and Nixon Administrations, wound up in that job after the ignominious defeat in Vietnam. Iraq looks like déjà vu all over again.

But Paul Wolfowitz, former Deputy Secretary of Defense, under Donald Rumsfeld, isn't dead yet.

As Neo-con in Chief, he did a yeoman job helping to engineering the Iraq war in 2003. His claim to fame was his ability to make the intelligence fit the policy. Wolfowitz was widely seen as one of the most hawkish of the neo-cons in the Republican Party.

In the fourth year of the Iraq war, Wolfowitz is left, with the rest of us, contemplating the catastrophe that he, and the Bush Administration has concocted.

He must have seen the handwriting on the wall and beat a hasty retreat with a little shove from his friends, leaving his neo-conservative colleagues there to pick up the pieces or look for another place to start a war, like Iran, perhaps.

So what will Wolfowitz's next adventure be? We can only surmise from his past history.

One example of where Wolfowitz was coming from—his appointment as Ambassador to the Republic of Indonesia from 1986–89 while General Suharto was its president, a period of turmoil when East Timor was trying to free itself from Indonesian rule.

Joseph Nevins, an assistant professor at Vassar College and author of a book on East Timor, says of Wolfowitz during that period: "He consistently argued against East Timorese self-determination, a position he maintained through 1999. While he sometimes criticized the Indonesian military's more high-profile atrocities, his opposition to any talk favoring an Indonesian withdrawal from East Timor—as demanded by the United

Nations—lent credibility to Indonesia's presence in East Timor, facilitating the very atrocities he occasionally decried."

ABC News reported that "thousands of leftists detained after the 1965 US—backed military coup that brought Suharto to power were still languishing in jail without trial." ABC News reported further that "tens of thousands of people in East Timor, a country Suharto's troops occupied in 1975, died during the 1980s in a series of army anti-insurgency offensives."

"Wolfowitz went to East Timor and saw abuses going on, but kept quiet," said Binny Buchori of the International NGO Forum on Indonesian Development.

In 1989, Paul Wolfowitz joined the administration of George Bush, 41, as Under-Secretary for Defense Policy which happened to be under then Secretary of Defense Dick Chaney, who is now Vice President Dick Chaney in the administration of George Bush, 43.

So Paul Dundes Wolfowitz has come full circle.

Centrifuging Iran

George W. Bush is not going to stand for Iran getting a "nucular" weapon. No Siree. He's not going to let it happen.

He has two US aircraft carriers and a flotilla of warships in the Persian Gulf right now, for previously unannounced exercises, playing military games, to see to it that Iran stops enriching uranium.

George Bush would like to think he can control the world's nuclear power.

But the genie is out of the bottle, and has been for some time. Let's review the bidding on the nuclear problem.

The United States didn't have a dog in the fight until December 7, 1941, Pearl Harbor day, after which the Manhattan Project went into full gear. It kicked off the race for an atomic weapon.

The United States demonstrated its victory in that race when it dropped "Little Boy" on Hiroshima on August 6, 1945 and "Fat Man" on Nagasaki on August 9th. It is estimated that 140,000 died in Hiroshima and roughly 74,000 in Nagasaki, mostly civilians.

That attack ended World War II with a bang so that the Cold War with the Soviet Union could begin with a whimper.

The United States was triumphal with its monopoly of the bomb and hugged the secret close to the chest. But it is in the nature of secrets to be exposed.

The Soviet Union exploded its first atomic weapon in August of 1949.

The Soviet Union had some good scientists, and whether they devised an atomic bomb on their own or stole the secret from us is still a matter of speculation. Scientific information has a way of proliferating.

Maybe they got a little help from a self-confessed stoolie, David Greenglass, a sergeant in the US Army assigned to the Manhattan Project. Judging from the sketch of the atom bomb that he showed to the FBI and claimed to have passed on to the Russians, it doesn't look as though he gave them very much. Nevertheless, he fingered his sister and brother-in-law, Ethel and Julius Rosenberg, who paid the ultimate price, executed as traitors to their country. Whether they were Soviet spies or just a couple of idealistic American communists, made scapegoats, may be debatable.

By January of 1950, President Harry Truman ordered the development of the hydrogen bomb and by November of '52 it was successfully tested.

True to form, in August of 1953, the Soviet Union tested its first hydrogen bomb.

And so it went. It wasn't long before the nuclear club was formed and the dance of death continued.

Currently, eight states have successfully detonated nuclear weapons, but the "Big Five", the United States, Russia (formerly Soviet Union), the United Kingdom, France and China are considered to be "nuclear weapons states", an internationally recognized status conferred by the Nuclear Non-Proliferation Treaty (NPT).

India, Pakistan and North Korea are non-signatory states of the NPT.

Israel is in a class by itself. It is widely believed to have an arsenal of more than 200 nuclear weapons, the only country in the Middle East to have them, but they don't want to talk about it, and we let them get away with that.

In 1977, when Saddam Hussein was developing a nuclear facility at Osirak, 11 miles southeast of Baghdad, Israel frowned upon the idea. In 1981, in a musically enhanced preventive strike, entitled Operation Opera, the plant was crippled by Israeli aircraft. The job was finished by American aircraft during the 1991 Gulf War.

Yes, this takes us to Iran, the magical Persian kingdom.

Iran has been enriching uranium. They don't deny it. They say it is for peaceful purposes. And nobody believes them. Why should they? Iran has plenty of oil. Why would they need nuclear power? Why don't they come clean and tell the truth. Just say, "We need nuclear weapons for defense. If you're a small nation, and you're not waving a ding-dong atom bomb around, you're likely to get hit by the US of A. Take a look at Iraq. Take a look at North Korea. We're the third wheel on the "axis of evil". Kim

Jong-il got his weapon just in time. Now the US is willing to talk politely with North Korea."

"Our people are not going to allow their nuclear rights to be seized," said Hashemi Rafsanjani, the former Iranian President. He insisted that Iran's decision to continue its nuclear program was irreversible and that his country could not be treated like Iraq. Furthermore, he threatened, western opposition to Iran's decision would cost them dearly.

Would George Bush take this as a threat? He said he was working on a diplomatic solution, but was skeptical that one could be found.

"The use of force is the last option for any president. You know we have used force in the recent past to secure our country," President Bush said. "All options are on the table."

When have you heard that before?

Guns and Butter

You don't have to be a rocket scientist or a professor of economics to know that wars and arms production can no longer keep a capitalist economy afloat as it did in the past. At one time, the military-industrial complex, as described by President Dwight Eisenhower, was the arbiter of the system. No more.

The productivity of labor has become so great with modern technology, that we can now have our guns and butter and then some. We have learned to live with war, considered by many as just another minor annoyance in our lives.

As we automate and cybernate and digitize, creating more and more superfluous people throughout the world, we drift inexorably into the worldwide economic crisis looming just ahead. So, what are we to do with all these superfluous people? If we don't change the system, they're going to take matters into their own hands and they'll find a way to change it. You can count on that. The immigrant marches across the country on May 1 showed the way. The people put their power where the problem is.

The contradictions of capitalism have reached critical mass. It's hard to tell which disaster will overtake us next. We have President Bush, with nuclear weapons, threatening Iranians who are feverishly trying to make their own. Is there a nuclear holocaust in our future? We have the possibility of another Katrina facing us as the new hurricane season begins in June. Intensified weather changes might put more than just the Gulf Coast in jeopardy.

There is an overwhelming consensus among scientists that global warning is upon us. Canaries in the mine are dying. The ice caps are melting. The polar bears are drowning. Yet our wonder-boy president continues to fight an imperialist war for hegemony and oil that does more than its share in contributing to the disaster of global warming. The Kyoto Treaty, an international agreement to reduce the emission of greenhouse gases and cut the use of fossil fuel, still not ratified by the United States.

We've faced critical situations like this before. With all the international tension, today, over Iran's current attempts at enriching uranium for producing power, as they say—or for a nuclear weapon, as we believe—it might be worth a look back at how it all started—the race for the development of atomic weapons at the start of World War II.

In 1939, Hitler was looking for that "secret weapon" that would insure his conquest of Europe and the world. Work with the isotopes of uranium was going on in Germany by some of that country's leading physicists, like Otto Hahn and Fritz Strassman, who happened to be Jewish. Hitler's anti-Semitism drove them, and other scientists, into exile where they continued their work on nuclear fission in Great Britain and the United States. Nice going, Adolf!

British Intelligence discovered, in 1942, that Hitler had two assets in occupied Norway that could get him an atomic weapon—one was a plant for producing heavy water, necessary at that time for enriching uranium, and the other was a nuclear physicist by the name of Niels Bohr, who knew how to do it. Britain's objective was to destroy the plant and convince Bohr to escape to the west, which he did.

All these physicists, working on the problem, knew it would take a massive effort to beat Hitler to the punch. It was Albert Einstein and Hungarian physicist, Leó Szilárd, who wrote that now famous letter to President Franklin Delano Roosevelt. Roosevelt recognized the need for a massive program of atomic research in the United States. That led to the creation of the Manhattan Project. The project eventually employed more than 130,000 people and cost $2 billion ($20 billion in current dollars). By 1945, with the war in Europe about over and Japan on the ropes, the Manhattan Project reached its goal, a working atom bomb, two of which, cutely named "Little Boy" and "Fat Man" were dropped on Hiroshima and Nagasaki.

Yes, we did stop Hitler, thanks mainly to the Red Army, and we did stop him from getting an atomic bomb. Unfortunately, we used ours needlessly, on two Japanese cities. President Harry Truman ordered the attacks, tarnishing his legacy forever.

What have we learned from this dire lesson? Not much, it seems. If we can put a man on the moon, why can't we impeach George Bush? It really wouldn't take resources the size of the Manhattan Project.

No need to go through the litany of reasons why he needs impeachment. There certainly are enough of them, not counting his lying us into war and violating the Fourth Amendment by spying on US citizens without a warrant.

The House of Representatives impeached Bill Clinton for far less. Most people don't even remember that it happened. His crime, lying about a sexual relationship with that woman. The Senate failed to follow up on the House's impeachment by not throwing Clinton out of the White House. Congress could make up for that indiscretion by getting rid of George Bush now.

> An anonymous blogger, **spd rdr,** put it this way:
> (With deepest apologies
> to Frank Sinatra)
>
> Now Hit the Highway
> (to the tune of "I Did It My Way")
>
> And now, the end is here,
> and so I'm gone,
> and so's your money.
> But friends,
> you shouldn't fear,
> I won't be back,
> Hey! That ain't funny.
> "You know,
> that George Bush lied",
> I've shouted each and every tirade.
> No more,
> no more of that,
> Now hit the highway!

Bush's Latin Slip

Bush put the bear-hug on Brazil's president, Lula da Silva, on the first leg of his vaunted South American trip. That picture, featured in the media, must have sent shivers up the spine of most Latinos.

The five nation tour of Brazil, Uruguay, Colombia, Guatemala, and Mexico, aims to improve the image of the colossus of the north but it may be having the opposite effect.

"I don't think America gets enough credit for trying to help improve people's lives" Mr. Bush said at a press conference in Sao Paulo.

Brazilians must feel otherwise. Protesters were out in force throughout the region, calling for the "gringo" to go home as well as calling Bush everything from a murderer, a fascist and a hypocrite. They also called him a warmonger and planet polluter. Polls show widespread opposition to the Iraq war and U.S. trade and immigration policies.

In Guatemala, anticipating Bush's arrival, a group of Mayan priests said they would "purify" a sacred site of "bad spirits" after Bush's scheduled visit.

While Bush was speechifying in Brazil, Venezuela's Hugo Chavez, Bush's nemesis, was holding a rally in Buenos Aires, Argentina, across the river from Montevideo, Uruguay, Bush's next port of call. He was condemning the ethanol plan that Bush and the Brazilian leader had devised for biofuels, accusing the United States of trying to "substitute the production of foodstuffs for animals and human beings with the production of foodstuffs for vehicles, to sustain the American way of life."

When in Colombia, Bush should make a side trip down to Putumayo and visit some coca plantations, the source of a lot of the cocaine that hits the streets of America. He might get a glimpse of the devastation caused by the spraying of Monsanto's Roundup plus—an herbicide, used against the coca crop (and every other plant it touches) as well as the *campesinos*, the peasants, living in the area. This offensive program has been supported by a whopping three billion of US tax dollars, in the last five years, funneled through the so-called "Plan Colombia", your bucks and mine marching off to the "war on drugs"—eighty percent of which was diverted and used to fight the FARC.

While in Colombia, President Bush might do well to visit with the FARC—Revolutionary Armed Forces of Colombia—People's Army—the leading guerrilla group in the country. Bush could even propose a summit meeting with Manuel Marulanda Veloz, leader of the FARC, since one day, perhaps in the not too distant future, the FARC might take over the country. That's been known to happen throughout history. (One day guerrilla, next day head of state, [sic] George Washington, Nelson Mandela, Menachem Begin)

Marulanda, also known as Tirofijo (Sureshot) might be willing to meet with the President even though in March of 2006, Albert Gonzalez, the Attorney General of the United States, announced, in conjunction with the DEA and Department of Justice officials, that the State Department had placed a five million dollar reward on Tirofijo's head, or information leading to his capture.

It is obvious that Bush avoided the one country he should have rated most important to include in a South American tour—Venezuela.

Venezuela provides the United States with one-sixth of its oil imports. It is also a country with enormous oil reserves—about 350 billion barrels if all the heavy and light crude are counted. A US Energy Department expert believes Venezuela holds 90% of the world's super-heavy tar oil reserves—an estimated total of 1.36 trillion barrels from which light oil can be extracted, at a higher but viable cost.

Sounds like Venezuela is a country with whom we should be friendlier, considering it could be the most important source of our future oil supply. But instead of taking that approach, the Bush Administration has made several attempts, some of them not so covert, to get rid of Chavez. No luck so far. Obviously, Bush will try again.

There is an old saying, "If you can't lick'em, join'em". But that may not be the way Bush sees it. From previous experience, it wouldn't be a stretch to figure that the US would go all out to get its hands on that oil—by war, if necessary, as it tried to do in Iraq. It undoubtedly would end up in the same kind of quagmire.

The shadow of Hugo Chavez lurks in the background as George Bush makes his frantic rounds, meeting with Latin American heads of state.

Chavez wants to make it clear that he has done more for the poorer Latin nations than the Bush Administration has. Bankrolled by more than $50 billion a year in oil earnings, Chavez has been dispensing cash around the region like a fairy godfather. He's bought up more than $3 billion worth of debt in Argentina, given economic aid to Bolivia and sold oil to his friends in the region at bargain basement prices.

The Bush Administration, on the other hand, has been more Scrooge than Santa Claus when dealing with Latin American nations. US aid to the region barely totaled a measly $1.7 billion this year—nearly half of that going to Colombia.

Small wonder than that Argentine President Nestor Kirchner has been cozy with Chavez, and Bolivia's Evo Morales, Ecuador's Rafael Correa and Nicaragua's Daniel Ortega have been giving Bush the bum's rush.

Remember the "Alliance for Progress"? In March of 1961, President John F. Kennedy proposed a ten-year economic plan for Latin America.

"… we propose to complete the revolution of the Americas," it said. "… to build a hemisphere where all men can hope for a suitable standard of living and all can live out their lives in dignity and in freedom …"

It worked well. JFK had the Latin countries eating out of his hand. There was no Hugo Chavez to gum up the works.

George Bush is no JFK. Maybe he shoulda stood in bed instead of taking this trip. This trip may well turn into a nasty slip.

DEMOCRATS' DILEMMA:
Back on the Table?

"Impeachment is off the table," said newly elected Democratic Speaker of the House, Nancy Pelosi, to reporter Leslie Stahl, on a *Sixty Minutes* broadcast.

Will the American people make George W. Bush pay the price for his war crimes in Iraq? We all know there is a barrel full of "high crimes and misdemeanors" that would make impeachment very constitutional.

After Bush's recent "surge" speech (21,500 more troops for Iraq), there has been a groundswell of opinion to get impeachment back on the table. Nancy is now pawing the ground when asked if she's changed her mind on the subject. She says she supports Congressional investigations into such areas as intelligence failures and Halliburton contracts but is still waffling on impeachment.

Will George W. Bush pay the price? I think not.

Let's go to the facts ...

Only three Presidents have ever faced impeachment in the history of this nation—Andrew Johnson in 1868, Richard Nixon in 1974 and Bill Clinton in 1998.

It's not easy to impeach a President. There are two stages in the process. It takes a majority of the House of Representatives to vote a bill of Impeachment but the Constitution requires a two-thirds vote of the Senate to convict.

Bill Clinton was hit with the bill of impeachment in the House, but the Senate didn't have the stomach to convict. After all, it was only for having oral sex with a White House intern. If it had been for his role in N.A.T.O's bombing Serbia back to the Stone Age during the Balkan war in 1999, we might have had a better chance.

Richard Nixon, of course, resigned before impeachment charges could be drawn up for the "third-rate burglary attempt" at the Watergate offices of the Democratic Party.

Andrew Johnson was impeached by the House of Representatives in 1868 over some hanky-panky with Reconstruction policy. There was still enough sentiment around for restoring slavery after the Civil War. But, again, the Senate wouldn't convict.

So what chance do we have of impeaching George W. Bush, even though his high crimes and misdemeanors, in both foreign and domestic policy, are in everyone's face? There might have been some chance if the Democratic Party weren't joined at the hip with the War Party. Every potential Democratic candidate for the presidency in 2008, so far, is too frightened or too cagey to call George Bush the imperial wizard or to call him naked. And the reasons for the Democrats' dilemma are laid out there like man-holes with their covers off.

Basically, we have a one party system in this country with two ugly faces.

There was a time when the Democratic Party allowed as how the working class deserved more than a few crumbs falling from the table. That was a time, of course, when the American labor movement had some "cojones", that was a time when John L. Lewis and the Reuther Brothers, Walter and Victor, organized the CIO and brought General Motors to its knees in the great sit-down strikes of 1936 and 1937. That was a time when President Franklin Roosevelt was known to say, "Clear it with Sidney" when an important issue involving labor came up—the "Sidney" being Sidney Hillman, a key union leader in the Democratic Party. But that was after the Great Depression. Will we have to go through that cycle again before we get some justice?

Where are the days when at least one of our political parties represented the majority of the people in this country—the working people, minorities, have-nots, recent immigrants, and the like?

Yes, we have a system problem here. Everybody's talking about how to get out of Iraq, but nobody is doing much to accomplish it. Books are being written about it. There is constant discussion about it on what is called TV news. Congress is regularly coming up with non-binding resolutions.

There might be a fooler in here, somewhere. Maybe all those talking about getting out of Iraq don't want to get out of Iraq. Congress gave George Bush a blank check to go to war in 2003, and most of the Democratic Party members voted for it—thereby giving up its exclusive constitutional right—the right to declare war. And by doing that it knocked "checks and balances" (cornerstone of American democracy) into a cocked hat.

Congress also has the power of the purse. They can still stop Bush by cutting off funding for the war. What! Cut off support for our troops while they're in harm's way? That will never happen and Bush knows it, so he can go his own way. He knows he has Congress by those same "cojones".

Let's get down to the nitty-gritty. We all know that war is a profit-making operation. Besides, Iraq is sitting on the second largest reserve of oil in the world. And the world is running out of the stuff real fast.

The Bush administration has no intention of leaving Iraq. According to the Chicago Tribune, US engineers are constructing 14 "enduring bases"—that's Pentagon-speak for long term encampments. There is also oil from the Caspian area to keep an eye on.

It's there for all to see.

Corporate America is an equal opportunity lobbyist, along with their one ally in the Middle East. They're strictly non-partisan. And their roots are deep in Congress. So, we're talking about the two wings of the capitalist structure. If we really want to make some changes, we should start examining that structure.

As a noted campaigner once said in a Clinton election, "It's the economy, Stupid!" Well, it's not just the economy.

It's the system, Stupid!

The Nation Asks

"Will the Progressive Majority Emerge?" The Nation Magazine asks, in its current issue (7/9/07) featuring a cover story by Rick Perlstein.

Perlstein proves, by the polls, that a progressive majority does, indeed, exist as measured by the public's stance on most major issues. But where is it hiding?

Will the progressive majority please stand up!

The problem is, Perlstein says, the Democrats are reluctant to pin a "Democratic label" on themselves, even though polls show that a majority of voters believe in the liberal principles of the Democratic Party.

Looks like we have a perception problem, here. Can The Nation straighten that one out?

The Nation has always been a classy magazine with a venerable history. I've had a subscription to it for as long as I can remember.

The Nation was founded in 1865 as an Abolitionist publication and is the oldest continuously published weekly magazine in the United States devoted to politics and culture. Today, it defines itself as "the flagship of the left."

(How far left, it's not saying)

In 1881, railroad baron Henry Villard acquired The Nation and converted it into a weekly literary supplement for his daily newspaper the New York Evening Post. In 1918, Villard's son, Oswald Garrison Villard, gave it a liberal orientation.

In its 142 year history, The Nation has had illustrious editors—Socialist Norman Thomas, Victor Navasky, Carey McWilliams, Freda Kirchwey, to name a few.

Contributors have included Albert Einstein, Martin Luther King, Jr., Gore Vidal, I.F. Stone, Leon Trotsky, John Steinbeck, Jean-Paul Sartre, and many, many more. Today, the magazine is supported by such luminary liberals as Paul Newman, Calvin Trillin and Alexander Cockburn. The current publisher and editor is Katrina vanden Heuvel.

Paradoxically, although coming from an old and staunch capitalist family, vanden Heuvel is married to New York University history professor, Stephen F. Cohen, an expert on the former Soviet Union. She should be conversant with the contradictions of capitalism.

So why are we stuck in trying to answer the question, "Will the Progressive Majority Emerge?" The answer is simple. Yes—when the economy tanks.

What we should be examining is how close we are to a crash and what must be done to avert one. In effect, how can we put our finger in the dike of capitalism.

Wall Street is an ostrich with its head in the sand. Yeah, the market's up … things are great … yeah, like they are in Iraq … how long can we keep this war going …

There are two nodal points we better watch—the war, and the upcoming presidential election. War and elections have raised havoc with economies in the past.

You could ask, "What might I.F. Stone or Leon Trotsky, have suggested in this tricky atmosphere?" That, of course, would be speculative. But we might come up with some answers.

How long can an economic system grow, when, in 2004, credit market debt reached 304% of gross domestic product? Apparently, financially servicing the American economy is more important than producing useful commodities. Non-productive parasites, as some Marxist economists have called them, undermine the economic system.

"No presidential clan has been so involved in banking, investment and money market management over so much time as the Bush clan," says Kevin Phillips in his book, "American Theocracy". "Lifetime patrons of George W. Bush are Morgan Stanley, Merrill Lynch, Pricewaterhouse-Coopers and MBNA, the credit card giant."

Phillips asserts that over the last part of the 20th century the federal government chose finance to be ascendant over manufacturing. America's productive sector—manufacturing—lost its markets, profits, and prime political access. In the final analysis, Phillips is looking at late stage capitalism, characterized by monopoly, war and end of empire.

These are some of the things I would also be looking for in the pages of The Nation Magazine. Sometimes we get lost in the skirts of the Democratic Party.

Where can this rotten-ripe economy go? Look through some prisms. Check out some scenarios.

China could, of course, pull its paper.

"To pay for the ongoing wars in Iraq and Afghanistan," says Ron Scherer of The Christian Science Monitor, "spending about $10 billion a month, the US used its credit card, counting on the Chinese and other foreign buyers of its debt to pay the bills."

But the Bush Administration is counting on the Chinese not to call in their debt, because if they did, they could bring on a world-wide economic collapse which would also swallow them.

As oil production peaks around the world, we could save ourselves with a crash course on the Marshall Plan, and see how fast we can develop alternative energy sources. We could spin off industries in wind and sun power, geothermal and wave technologies that could give dying capitalism a new lease on life.

But will we have the motivation to do it—the strength to fight off the death-grip of the expiring petroleum giants? I can't believe that we'd fight to the death to grab the last shrinking pools of oil on the planet.

It would be a race to the finish. What will get us first? Will it be energy starvation or global warming?

The Nation Magazine will be there to chronicle the event.

Break it Up!

No, I'm not talking about Iraq, the Sunnis, the Shiites and the Kurds, or the feud in Congress over non-binding resolutions. I'm talking about the United States of America.

Does that shock you? Well, the idea of breaking it up is being toyed with by none other than Governor Arnold Schwarzenegger of California and delineated by Gar Alperevitz, professor of political economy at the University of Maryland, in an Op-Ed piece in the New York Times. (2/10/2007) And they're not talking about states' right vs. the federal government's centralized power. That was a conflict that went on for most of our history.

"California's governor", the professor says, "has put his finger on a little discussed flaw in America's constitutional formula. The United States is almost certainly too big to be a meaningful democracy ... sooner or later, a profound, probably regional, decentralization of the Federal system may be all but inevitable."

We have to destroy the system to save it.

In land mass, the United States is 6,092,510.8 square miles and I presume that just includes the 50 states. It's about half the size of Russia; about three-tenths the size of Africa; about half the size of South America (or slightly larger than Brazil); slightly larger than China; almost two and a half times the size of the European Union. We have a population of 298,444,215 people.

One characteristic of "bigness" is that the big or bigger nations are always beating up on smaller ones. They never pick on someone their own size. And in most cases they usually lose the wars that they start.

So, not only does might not make right, but the mighty ones rarely get what they go after. Witness Iraq. The United States (a big nation) went to war against Iraq (a small nation) presumably to get rid of weapons of mass destruction (which they didn't have) and fight terrorists that were presumably hiding out in that country (which they weren't). But terrorists (or freedom fighters) are there, in force, now, and the punditry says we have already lost the war.

The Air Forces Journal calls this the David and Goliath effect.

In his book, *Small Wars*, British Army Col. C.E. Callwell warned that a powerful force stands to lose an asymmetric fight "if it is unable to draw the enemy insurgents into a head-on battle. Insurgents adapt their strategy and tactics to capitalize on the weaknesses of their larger foe."

Is Governor Schwarzenegger talking about California breaking away because he wants the mother country to be less belligerent; or, since he can't be president of the USA (as a foreign born, naturalized citizen) he wants to be a bigger fish in a smaller pond?

Schwarzenegger says, "We (California) are the modern equivalent of the ancient city-states of Athens and Sparta. We have the economic strength; we have the population and the technological force of a nation-state. We are a good and global commonwealth."

Maybe he can get away with that opinion since be brought Britain's Prime Minister, Tony Blair, to the Port of Long Beach, California, last year, to sign and accord between California and Britain on global warming. I suppose that gives California "nation" status.

Once California breaks away, other states or regions are sure to follow. There's enough dissatisfaction with the Federal government to go around. We don't have to go all the way to the formation of separate states. If we did that, we'd start fighting with each other. We could be a federation of regions. It would be harder for any region to start a war with another region or another country for that matter.

Nevada, I think should unhinge and amalgamate with California since Los Angeles and Las Vegas are a good pairing, joined as they are by the umbilical cord of Interstate 15.

The original 13 colonies would make a good grouping, but they should be split into northern and southern regions. New England—Massachusetts, Connecticut, Rhode Island, plus New York, New Jersey, Pennsylvania, Delaware and Maryland make up an ideal region. The southern originals, Virginia, North and South Carolina, Georgia and Florida would do the same.

Maine was originally annexed to Massachusetts and didn't become a state until March 3, 1820 as a result of the Missouri Compromise. Maine was the free state to offset the slave state, Missouri, to balance the number of states on either side of the Mason-Dixon line. Vermont, the Green Mountain state, was the 14th to join the Union. It derived its name from the French "Vert Mont".

The Great Lake states of Minnesota, Wisconsin. Michigan, Ohio, Indiana and Illinois have a common interest in the weather and would be suitable to make up another grouping in the newly formed federation of the former United States of America.

The same would hold true of North and South Dakota, Montana and Wyoming, the wheat and cowboy states; as would the Pacific Northwest states of the Lewis and Clark expedition, Washington, Oregon and Idaho.

The four-corner states of Utah, Colorado, Arizona and New Mexico are a natural set. Appalachia—Tennessee, Kentucky and the deep-south states of Arkansas, Mississippi, Alabama and Louisiana would go together.

That leaves Texas and Oklahoma hanging out there by themselves. We could hook Oklahoma to Texas and call it the Lone Star Region.

Reconstituted in this manner, the former United States of America could finally heed the warning of the former General and President Dwight D. Eisenhower, "beware the military-industrial complex." In fact, under the new setup, of smaller, more efficient federated regions, we can get rid of the military-industrial complex completely. Who needs them? We can even make any kind of military establishment illegal and thereby save the trillions and trillions of dollars wasted on wars.

Using that money, we can build a truly fantastic society.

One Fell Into the Cuckoo's Nest

The class struggle is alive but not very well in New York City.

The leader of the recent 60-hour transit strike is a man by the name of Roger Toussaint, namesake of Toussaint L'Ouverture, the legendary hero of the Haitian revolution whose name literally means, "he who can find an opening."

One would think that Mayor Michael Bloomberg would have opened his arms and invited Toussaint in to "find an opening" for a settlement, before they called this strike that froze the toes of so many New Yorkers.

Instead, the billionaire Mayor got the courts to fine the union *a million dollars a day* and furthermore he would not allow negotiations to begin anew until the transit workers were back at work. So early in the game? In the United States of America, negotiations continue while the strike goes on. That's the way to arrive at a fair settlement. Otherwise, it's called a capitulation.

Then the Mayor, within those same 60 hours, threatened to have the union leaders jailed and each worker fined for each day missed. And this, over a 4 cent to the dollar increase in the pension plan formula for newly hired workers. How measly can a billion dollar mayor be? He insulted the people who drive New York City's trains and buses, the people responsible for the public's well-being and safety, and for getting them to work on time—he called them "thugs" and from his billionaire perch, he called them "selfish"—people living from paycheck to paycheck, scrabbling to make a living. What was he trying to do? Cause a race riot? A large percentage of transit workers are black or brown. The Mayor is beginning to sound more and more like the President.

Roger Toussaint, the man who can find an opening, said transit workers would go back to work if management took the pension question off the table and let negotiations continue.

Roger found that "opening". The MTA (Metropolitan Transport Authority) hinted it would take the pension issue off the table. Toussaint quickly ordered his people back to work—and not a moment too soon.

Both sides managed to save a little face. Not only was Toussaint trying to fight the entrenched power of the State, but he also had his own parent organization, the International Transport Workers Union against him! So Roger beat a hasty retreat.

Not a single Democrat came out in support of the transit workers. Senator Hilary Rodham Clinton, touted candidate for the Presidency, said she was neutral and supported the Taylor Law that makes striking against the State or City government illegal. (questionably unconstitutional)

The three horsemen of the metropolis, billionaires Mayor Michael Bloomberg and MTA chairman Peter Kalikow and their media buddy, billionaire Rupert Murdoch, dictator of Fox News and the New York Post, had no qualms lecturing the transit workers on the need to tighten their belts.

The strike may be over but there is a festering open wound and this, for certain, will flare again. Where and when? Any place, any time.

This 60-hour transit strike demonstrates a deeper reality, the working class is there and it wants to fight. The transit workers, and all of labor have learned a bitter lesson. It can't count on its so-called political friends nor its corrupt leadership. It has to forge new weapons. Each generation of American workers has to bring new tactics to the changing technology of production. In the 1930s it was the sit-ins, in the 1960s, the marches.

There have been other comparable events in the annals of labor history when local unions had to fight against their own internationals. The confrontation between Jimmy Hoffa and Farrell Dobbs is a good example. Farrell Dobbs and the Dunn Brothers, members of the Socialist Labor Party, ran Teamster Local 544 in Minneapolis in 1941.

"One of the outstanding things," Farrell Dobbs had said, "is not only the courage but the resourcefulness that a body of workers show when they're in a mood to fight and they have leaders who are willing to lead them into a fight."

At that time, Dan Tobin was President of the International Brotherhood of Teamsters and a close friend of President Franklin D. Roosevelt. The war in Europe was raging and there was heavy pressure on Roosevelt to get the US into it. President Roosevelt did not want Socialists in powerful labor positions during wartime and he asked his friend, Tobin, to do something about it. Tobin ordered Hoffa to have the International take over the Minneapolis Local 544 and get rid of Farrell Dobbs and the Dunne Brothers.

"Now, it is true that Hoffa led the goon squads sent into Minneapolis against Local 544," Farrell Dobbs said, "but Hoffa says that he whipped us. Now, it's a little more complicated than that. He got a little help from his friends, like the Minneapolis Police Department, the courts of the city, the county and the state, the Mayor and the Governor and an anti-labor law that had been rigged and put through the Legislature—and by the FBI and the US Department of Justice and Franklin Delano Roosevelt, who then happened to be President of the United States, so you've got to admit, Hoffa had just a little help, didn't he?"

And so did Michael Bloomberg. New York's 60-hour transit strike ripped the mask away and revealed the face of power and what that means for organized labor and for the unorganized. It showed the inadequacies of labor unions in the fight against those arrayed against them. The lack of a political structure leaves them defenseless against continuous attacks.

Labor, organized and unorganized, and its natural allies better start working to regain its former strength within the Democratic Party (which now appears hopeless) or start a party of its own that will keep us all out of the Cuckoo's Nest. Maybe one with a socialist orientation, with an anti-capitalist political agenda will do the trick.

In New York's aborted transit strike, its leader, Roger Toussaint succeeded in finding an opening. Unfortunately he, himself, fell through it—into the Cuckoo's Nest.

Third Party Gambit

We, the people of the United States of America, with a great tradition of third party movements, need a major third political party, and we need it now, because the leadership of the two major parties, Bush Administration Republicans and the Democrats' Leadership Council are corrupt to the core and not fulfilling the needs of the people. Changes must be made before it's too late.

If most members of Congress are not in the pocket of one American corporate interest, or another, they're beholden to an alien interest and aren't even registered as agents of a foreign power. Elections have become a race for big bucks, sort of an auction among the big guys.

We must act now. Let's go back to the beginning. Call it "The Democratic-Republican Party."

Thomas Jefferson and James Madison created The Democratic-Republican Party in 1792 to oppose Alexander Hamilton's Federalist Party, which supported the interests of the bankers.

The Democratic-Republicans supported the small farmers over bankers, industrialists, merchants and other monied interests. And that's the sort of thing we need today.

We can do it again. Third parties have had successes and failures throughout our history, but whichever, they've contributed to the dialogue of democracy and kept our political system vibrant.

The first successful third party was The Whig Party, formed in 1833. Its membership was made up of famous names we learned in school—Daniel Webster, William Henry Harrison, Henry Clay, to name a few. They formed the party to oppose the policies of then-President Andrew Jackson. They felt about Jackson the way liberals, today, feel about George W. Bush. They favored Congress over the Executive Branch.

The first Whig elected President was William Henry Harrison in 1841 probably more because of his catchy campaign slogan, "Tippecanoe and Tyler, Too" than anything else; Tippecanoe being the battle he won against Tecumseh in the Indian Wars; Tyler being his vice-presidential running mate.

The Whigs faded away with Millard Fillmore in the 1850s but not before making a fight to end the expansion of slavery into the territories.

In the spring of 1864, during the darkest days of the Civil War, The National Union Party was created from elements of the Republicans and Democrats to re-elect Lincoln to a second term. The Radical Republicans didn't think Lincoln was competent enough to be run again. Lincoln selected Andrew Johnson as his running mate. Johnson became the 17th President of the United States when Lincoln was shot in 1865.

Another third party, running on steroids, was The Bull Moose Party. It was really The United States Progressive Party of 1912. It was formed by Theodore Roosevelt when he lost the Republican nomination to William Howard Taft. He walked out of the convention in a fit of anger and pulled his delegates with him. When reporters suggested that he wasn't fit for office, he shouted, "I'm as fit as a bull moose!" thereby giving his party a name that stuck. However, he lost the Republican nomination to Taft but ran on his own Bull Moose ticket in the 1912 election. Although Roosevelt lost, he split the Republican vote giving the victory to the Democrat, Woodrow Wilson.

Oh, well, that's American politics. Let's get a dog into this fight.

Where is Eugene Debs, now that we really need him?

Debs was one of the founders of the International Labor Union, which came to be known as the IWW or the "Wobblies".

In 1893, Debs organized the American Railway Union (ARU), one of the first industrial unions in the United States. When the ARU decided to strike the Pullman Palace Car Company, Debs warned against it. The union was too weak. But the ARU went ahead with a wildcat strike and brought traffic west of Chicago to a halt.

The Federal government intervened and sent troops in to break the strike on the grounds that it was hindering delivery of the mail. A supersized mêlée ensued. During the course of the strike, 13 strikers were killed and 57 were wounded. Six thousand rail workers did an estimated 80 million dollars' worth of property damaged, and Debs was found guilty of interfering with the mail and sent to prison. While in prison, he read the works of Karl Marx and came out a socialist.

Debs was a candidate for President of the United States five times, once on the Social Democratic Party ticket in 1900, then on the Socialist Party of America ticket in 1904, 1908, 1912 (running against T. Roosevelt, Taft and Wilson). In the 1920 election, still incarcerated, Debs ran from the Atlanta Penitentiary and pulled close to a million votes. On December 25, 1921, Christmas Day, President Warren G. Harding commuted Debs' sentence to time served.

Debs told an audience in Utah in 1910: "… if you are looking for a Moses to lead you out of this capitalist wilderness, you will stay right where you are … you must use your heads as well as your hands, and get yourselves out of your present condition."

Debs' statement to the judge at his sentencing hearing was paraphrased by Tom Joad, Steinbeck's character in "The Grapes of Wrath": "Your Honor, years ago I recognized my kinship with all living beings, and I made up my mind that I was not one bit better than the meanest on earth. I said then, and I say now, that while there is a lower class, I am in it, and while there is a criminal element, I am of it, and while there is a soul in prison, I am not free."

Well, we don't have Gene Debs to run for us anymore. We'll have to make up our own slate for the *New* Democratic-Republican Party.

I nominate:

- Bill Moyers—for President of the United States. He's had White House experience under Lyndon Johnson and he played a key role in organizing and supervising the 1964 "Great Society" legislative task force.

- Al Gore—for Vice-President. He's held the job before, so he's experienced, and he can spend all the time he needs working on the problem of global warming.

- Keith Olbermann—for White House Press Secretary. He could certainly whip a group of reporters into shape (as well as the rest of the White House).

- Cindy Sheehan—for Secretary of State. She knows compassion and diplomacy. She's had a diplomatic duel with Bush of the White House since her son, Casey, was killed in Iraq, and she is relentless in her efforts to find out why. Also, let's keep the tradition of a woman in the job.

- Scott Ritter—for Secretary of Defense. He's a former Marine and was a member of the UN weapons of mass destruction search team in Iraq and found none. So he wouldn't have taken us into war.

- Michael Moore—for Secretary of Health and Human Services. With his film "SiCKO", he's making the Health Insurance Industry blush.

- Ralph Nader—for Secretary of Transportation. His book, "Unsafe at Any Speed" took Chevvie's Corvair apart and forced the auto industry to learn the word "safety". (He deserves a seat in the cabinet for his other work, too.)

- Bill Gates and Steve Jobs—for Secretaries of Energy. They should share that job for giving us the computer and saving all that energy.

- Howard Zinn—for Secretary of Education. What better choice than the man who wrote "A People's History of the United States.

- Patrick Fitzgerald—for Secretary of Justice. He successfully prosecuted Scooter Libby. Now, maybe we can get him to go after Karl Rove and Dick Cheney.

- Dennis Kucinich—for Delegate to the United Nations. He's a man with a world view even if he did come from Cleveland. We could give him a handlebar mustache.

- Paul Newman—to head up the Food and Drug Administration. He's earned millions for charity with his food products. If it's a "Newman's Own" you know it's good.

- Barbara Ehrenreich—for Secretary of Commerce. Having lived on minimum wage around the country, researching her book, and written "Nickel and Dimed" she knows the value of a buck.

There's your slate … You take it from here.

Recapitulation

On Thursday, May 3rd, the 10 Republican Party candidates for President held their first pre-primary live television campaign debate at the Reagan Library in Simi Valley, California, moderated by Chris Matthews of NBC.

At one point in the debate, Chris asked the candidates to raise there hands if they believed in evolution. Three of the 10 failed to raise their hands, proclaiming their lack of belief in evolution. They were Senator Sam Brownback of Kansas, Representative Tom Tancredo of Colorado and Governor Mike Huckabee of Arkansas.

Ontogeny recapitulates phylogeny. That's a fancy way of saying that the development of the individual of all species fully repeats the evolutionary development of that species. It's biological theory. Each successive stage in the development of an individual represents one of the adult forms that appeared in its evolutionary history. In eight weeks after fertilization, a single human embryo traces our entire evolutionary past. It's called the theory of evolution. Do you get that, Mike, Tom and Sam?

In their case, we might say that ignorance recapitulates stupidity. Are any of these the kind of guy we want for President?

But their position on evolution is not about thinking disabilities; it's about casting the net for votes. We all know that a sizable portion of our population has been dumbed down and deliberately so. I don't mean to get personal but a sizable portion of the sizeable portion are citizens of the rightward persuasion. That's a serious charge. I can only rely on the facts.

One method of dumbing down the population is to make political issues of "social issues" like abortion, school prayer, gay marriage, and other so-called "family values", major crusades of the religious right. "Creationism" is right wing chic. It turns us 180 degrees and takes us backward so that we have to retry the Scopes monkey trial of 1925. That's a show stopper.

The Scopes trial tested a state law in Tennessee that forbade the teaching of "any theory that denies the story of the Divine Creation of man as taught in the Bible".

John Scopes, a high school teacher, was arrested for teaching evolution from a chapter in a text book based on ideas developed from those set forth in Charles Darwin's "The Origin of Species".

The trial lasted eight days and after nine minutes of deliberation, the jury found Scopes guilty; but these were eight days that shook the world and provided the greatest show on earth before or since Barnum and Bailey, with chimps performing on the courthouse lawn.

The legal gymnastics of prosecutor William Jennings Bryan and defense attorney Clarence Darrow during the trial and the eventual appeal to the Supreme Court of Tennessee was full of sound and fury signifying nothing, and did little to change things.

The best thing to come out of that famous trial, made infamous by fictionalized accounts, was the 1955 Broadway play *Inherit the Wind*, staring Paul Muni and the hit Hollywood movie version, by the same name, in 1960, with Spencer Tracy and Frederick March as the dueling attorneys. The public probably learned more about evolution from these two dramas than they ever did from the event, itself.

Did Mike, Tom or Sam see either of these fictional versions of the trial? If they did, they might have learned something. They don't believe in evolution, yet each wants to be President of the United States.

But this is only one example of the dumbing down of America.

There is the sheer neglect of public education, its infrastructure, its physical plant as well as its teaching standards.

Parents, who can afford it, send their children to private school these days. And even some local areas, where the schools are so bad, the local government issues vouchers to some children so that they can attend better private schools. This is a country where good, free public education has always been a hallmark of a free democratic society.

Another example, the sell-out of our mainstream media. The big six media conglomerates, namely, AOL Time Warner, Disney, Viacom, News Corp. Ltd, Tele-Communications, Inc. and Westinghouse own all the major movie stud_os, all the TV networks, most of the music companies, and the important cable-TV channels. They control most of what we see, hear and read.

Commercial radio and television programs have became even more marinated in advertising than ever. Such a concentration of media power into so few hands violates every known theory of a free marketplace of ideas in a democracy.

Speaking of thinking abilities or disabilities, what can we say about our current leaders? The Bush Administration has attacked the very soul of American democracy, the first ten amendments to our Constitution, our "Bill of Rights". And how has George Bush done it? With something called the Patriot Act. What an insult to the country and every citizen.

How should a patriot act?

The immediate thing a patriot should do is insist that his Congressional Representatives in the House and in the Senate start impeachment proceedings against President Bush and Vice President Cheney for high crimes and misdemeanors (of which there are many) and simultaneously cut off all funding for war in Iraq except for the costs of protecting our troops by bringing them home.

Fate of the Democrats

In the fateful election of 2008, let's hope we don't see a replay of days gone by. If the leading Democratic candidates are destined to be Hillary Clinton or Baraka Obama, or John Edwards or one of the others following right behind, they all seem to be playing the numbers game so early in their careers. When do we get out of Iraq? In six months? Maybe a year? End of 2008?

Hillary Clinton is slicing the bacon very thin. "Anything Bush can do, she can do better …"

In the old days, they were called the "social democrats". They've been around a long time. They're an old international bunch. In Europe, before World War I, they were part of the Second International (SI). Why did they call themselves that? I suppose to distinguish themselves from the First and the Third. They claimed to believe in socialism achieved by democratic means. They could have stopped World War I before it started if they voted no funds for war in their respective nations. But they didn't. In the end, they went with their war parties. And we know what that cosmic clash brought upon us.

That's always been characteristic of the social democrats. They developed the technique of playing Tweedledee and Tweedledum with great skill and with the "running dogs", the main stream media, at their side, they were very effective. They always held up their part of the bargain. The system always had a hard time keeping the populous in line, the liberals, the so-called progressives, the minorities, the working class, and the labor movement (when we had one). Their aim: to reform the system and mitigate some of its more obvious depredations.

There always used to be a place for these disparate elements under the Democratic Party's big tent. Something for everyone, if only a few crumbs. And when that failed, there was always a third party or two around to absorb the disaffection.

Bill Clinton changed all that. He hired political consultant Dick Morris to manage his 1996 campaign for re-election. He bought into Morris' "triangulation" strategy which was to ignore your base and steal the other party's votes. It worked just fine and Bill won the election.

Now, Hillary is trying the triangulation strangulation formula. Don't let a good thing go to waste.

If the assault on the Democratic base began with the Ronald Reagan "Revolution" breaking the back of the air traffic controllers union (PATCO) in 1981, the process continued through the administrations of Bush (41), Clinton (42), and Bush (43) as unions were picked away and jobs outsourced to overseas labor pools where it's been a race to the bottom. The percentage of union members within the private sector, remaining in the United States, has declined from 15.5% in 1984 to just 7.9% in 2004.

With their base dwindling, what should a Democrat do if he or she has to look for votes in all the wrong places?

First, stop acting like a social democrat.

More that 70% of the electorate made their message loud and clear in the last election. They want the US out of Iraq, now! Congressional Democrats have the mandate of their constituencies and the constitutional power to do just that, now! Except for the funds needed to bring troops home, they can cut off funding for this war (as well as any other war—such as an attack on Iran, for one). Democrats in this Congress can do what their predecessors, prior to World War I, failed to do—withhold funds. There is no excuse in "we'll be accused of not supporting our troops when they're in harms way".

Democrats can also restore the constitutional rights of Americans. We're living in violation of the Geneva Conventions, Habeas Corpus and the Bill of Rights, notably the First and Fourth Amendments. How should a patriot act? Repeal the Patriot Act.

Should Hillary Clinton be elected, she owes a lot to this country. She and Bill are, singly and together, responsible for withholding Universal

Health Insurance from becoming the law of the land when they had the chance. They could have done it. In 1993, the president appointed his wife to head the Task Force on National Health Care Reform. The recommendation of the task force became known as the Clinton health care plan. The time was ripe but they were too frightened of single payer. They owed too much to Big Pharma and Big Insurance. The Health Industry's counter-attack, featuring the infamous "Harry and Louise" TV commercial, called the plan a travesty against "middle class values". That was the end of Clinton's attempt at reforming health care as he did "welfare as we knew it".

We can't afford to sit around doodling. We've got the big bad wolf knocking on the door.

I know a man who said, "It's shocking to see a door that's standing open, not swinging on its hinges but swinging on its lock, and the difference between which side it's swinging on is the difference between freedom and tyranny".

Brainless in Gaza

✦

(with apologies to Aldous Huxley, author of Eyeless in Gaza and John Milton, who coined the phrase in 1667)

Last June 27th, Israeli forces bombed a power plant in Gaza destroying a 140-megawatt reactor that supplied electricity and pumped water for two-thirds of Gaza's 1.4 million residents. Not only did this create a humanitarian disaster for the people of Gaza but also a catch-22 for the United States. The plant was insured by a US government agency for 48 million dollars.

Paying the claim on the plant would fly in the face of US policy to cut funding for all infrastructures in the Palestinian territories, zestfully announced last January, after the militant group, Hamas, won legislative elections.

All of that was overshadowed by the joint venture of the US and Israel in destroying Lebanon's infrastructure in July of 2006. In a heartless campaign, the US played a role slightly more than despicable. The United States delegation stalled a cease-fire in the UN Security Council long enough to give Israel the time to finish the job of demolishing Beirut. If the intention was to eliminate Hamas, it didn't succeed. The conflict killed over 1,200 people, displaced nearly 975,000 Lebanese. Even after the ceasefire, much of Southern Lebanon remained uninhabitable due to unexploded cluster bombs.

Israel is the only ally of the United States in the Middle East. And the two nations have a very special relationship. This is true. No matter what action Israel takes against the Palestinians, the US government's official line is, "Israel has the right to defend itself."

Maybe the US government has a hidden agenda. If the US government thinks it can use Israel to do its dirty work, perhaps it can work the other way as well. It could be a case of the tail wagging the dog.

The Iraq war is a good example. It certainly wasn't in the interests of the United States. There were no weapons of mass destruction there. They lied about that. There was no connection between Saddam Hussein and Al Qaida. They lied about that. And there was no link between Osama bin Laden and Saddam Hussein. They lied about that. Iraq posed no threat to the United States.

But Israel wanted Saddam Hussein out of the way, and the US was intent on obtaining permanent military bases in the Middle East to control the waning amount of oil reserves in that area and in the Caspian region. The United States military now has fourteen permanent bases in Iraq and the US is not about to pull its troops out of the country no matter what Congress or Cindy Sheehan say. The United States can use Israel as a watchdog over these bases.

Israel did prove its value, in 1981, when it took out an Iraqi nuclear reactor in Osirik, south-east of Bagdad, in a pre-emptive strike that just about killed Saddam's nuclear hopes. The US finished the job in the 1991 Gulf War. One hand washes the other.

Arab leaders have been calling for the elimination of Israel from the very beginning.

Israel has a population of a little over 6 million. The 22 nations that make up the Arab world have a combined population of 323 million. Doesn't this tell you something? It tells me that if I wished to live among Arabs, I would strive greatly to do so in peace and harmony.

The Jewish people, biblically "the chosen people", are noted for their intelligence, know-how, friendliness and compatibility. I heard it said, many times, after the State of Israel was formed, that the Israelis would "make the desert bloom". And they did—for Israel. In fact, Theodor Herzl, founder of the Zionist movement, wrote about the possibility of a harmonious partnership of Jews, Arabs and Christians in which Jewish capital and expertise would transform Palestine from its third world status into an advanced society where all would benefit.

So what happened? On November 29, 1947, the United Nations General Assembly voted for a Partition Plan that created the State of Israel in British mandated Palestinian territory. The British relinquished their mandate over Palestine in 1948. The Palestinians refused to accept the Partition Plan. War broke out immediately between the Arabs and the Jews. The Jews won the war, hands down, and the State of Israel became a fact of life. Israel then drew its own borders; including fifty percent more land than the UN Partition Plan allotted them. This is known as the Green Line. The Gaza Strip and the West Bank were left for the Palestinians after Egypt and Transjordan (now known as Jordan) withdrew.

Did Israel extend the hand of friendship (as in Herzl's vision) and if it was offered, was it not accepted by the Palestinians? It seems so, because the internecine warfare begun in 1948 has persisted, in one form or another, ever since.

Now we are facing a new situation.

Will it be Israel, the Bush Administration, or the newly elected US president in the next administration, who will order the pre-emptive strike on Iranian nuclear facilities? The thrust of the propaganda campaign now in full force indicates that all options are on the table.

The more things change, the more they remain the same.

Lies, Lies and More Lies ...

Is it true that Governments lie? Are you shocked—shocked to hear that! Well don't be. It's not unusual. People who take power, elected or otherwise, are usually alphas (Type A personalities) and their basal ganglia comes to the fore. It's as old as "civilization" itself. Napoleon. Julius Caesar, Alexander the Great. George W. Bush. We the people, with our rational cerebral cortexes don't always know how to cope with it.

"Remember the Maine!" That was a battle cry in 1898. The rest of it went: "To Hell With Spain!"

The *Maine*, a second class battleship of the US fleet, was lolling in the harbor of Havana, Cuba, "to protect American interests", and supposedly sending a message to the Spanish who were there protecting their colony from rebellious Cubans.

One calm and peaceful night, the *Maine* blew up and sank, killing 266 American sailors and injuring 60. The newly dubbed "yellow press" of Hearst's *New York Journal* and Pulitzer's *World*, viciously competing for headlines, jumped on the story, and started the litany, *Remember the Maine! To Hell with Spain*, a catchy phrase. It wasn't long before the American public was stoked up enough to cheer their government on into war with Spain.

The *casus belli*, used by President William McKinley, was a trumped up story that the Spanish had planted an explosive mine under the ship, but later investigation revealed that the explosion was probably the result of a coal bunker fire touching off some explosive ammunition in the hold. More skeptical people, however, believed that the *Maine* was sacrificed to rally public opinion against Spain. (Sound familiar?)

We had the war. Cuba became independent, though economically tied to the United States. It left us the glorious icon of Teddy Roosevelt charging, with his Rough Riders, up San Juan Hill. We continued the war with

Spain in the Philippines until we took that country, too. It started us on the road to Empire.

Another floating example of a government lie—the shenanigans in the Gulf of Tonkin in August of 1964.

A US destroyer was nosing around off the coast of North Vietnam (gathering intelligence?) when it was, reportedly, fired upon by North Vietnamese gunboats. President Lyndon Johnson ordered retaliatory action against the gunboats after "renewed attacks". But there were no renewed attacks.

The mainstream media, always anxious not to let facts get in the way, and with a bigger story on the horizon, did their usual thing. In this case it was the *New York Times* and the *Los Angeles Times* (big guns in the world of journalism) that picked up the battle cry. Both papers took the government propaganda handout and ran with it.

"By reporting official claims as absolute truths, American journalism opened the floodgates for the bloody Vietnam war," said *Fair,* the magazine of "Fairness and Accuracy in Media."

Congress, of course, played its role. The Gulf of Tonkin Resolution. The resolution authorized the President to "take all necessary measures to repel any armed attack against the forces of the United States and to prevent further aggression." (Sound familiar?)

Columnist Sydney Schanberg, prescient at the time, said, "We Americans are the ultimate innocents. We are forever desperate to believe that this time the government is telling us the truth."

Another maritime incident? You could call this one the "granddaddy" of them all. Pearl Harbor.

By December, 1941, the war in Europe was going badly. The Axis—Germany, Italy and Japan—were riding high. Hitler had most of Western Europe under his heel. In the Far East, Japan was working its way through the islands of the South Pacific.

There was enormous pressure on Roosevelt to bring the US into the war and save Britain and the Continent. The American temper was mixed. The America First Committee was strong and Nazi propagandists were invading the campuses of American colleges and universities.

Most Democrats, I, for one, do not want to believe that my hero, President Franklin Delano Roosevelt, had prior knowledge of that dastardly attack by the Japanese on that day that will live in infamy, December 7, 1941.

Well, there are "conspiracy theories" out there that say that he did. And there is reason to believe that perhaps they are true. What an irrefutable rationale for getting us into the war!

The mitigating circumstance is that he didn't know it would be such a massive force.

How about Korea in 1950? That was a neat one. It wasn't even called a war. It was a "police action". It precluded any need for a lie since the takeover was under the aegis of the newly created United Nations.

Korea, which had been under Japanese occupation from 1910 until 1945 and the end of World War II, was split at the 38th Parallel—the Soviet Union (with a little help from its friend, Red China) occupied the North—the United States taking over the South. When the occupying forces on both sides finally withdrew, they left a Communist regime in Pyongyang (North Korea) and a "democratic", or shall we say, a "non-Communist" regime in Seoul (South Korea). No peace treaty was ever signed. It remains that way to this very day.

We went to war against Iraq in 1991. We called it Operation Desert Storm. Saddam Hussein had invaded Kuwait.

Here again, we made it a UN action, recruiting a magnificent coalition. No lying necessary, but perhaps a bit of manipulation—signaling through diplomatic language an American "green light" for Saddam's Kuwaiti takeover. Before the invasion, Saddam had summoned the US Ambassador, April Glaspie, to his office, for a meeting. In the version published in the *New York Times* on September 23, 1990, Ambassador Glaspie is quoted as saying, "*We have no opinion on the Arab-Arab conflicts, like your border disagreement with Kuwait.*"

Saddam must have taken it as a "yes, go ahead". And he did. After all, the US was his friend and supporter during his eight-year war with Iran in the 1980s. Kissinger had said, at that time, we "tilt" toward Iraq. Rumsfeld was caught on camera shaking Saddam's hand.

When the tables turned and we were no longer friends, then President, at the time, George Herbert Walker Bush (41) launched Operation Desert Storm, otherwise known as the first Gulf War. But George, the elder, (with the advice of General Colin Powell) knew when to stop. He had sense enough to know that taking Baghdad would open a can of worms. Why didn't his son, President George Walker Bush (43) learn that lesson?

So here we are—in 2006—three and half years after the second invasion of Iraq, listening to lies, lies, and more lies....

Let George Do it

The government is outsourcing just about everything, reports The New York Times (2/3/07). Four hundred billion dollars was paid last year to independent contractors to do jobs that, traditionally and rightly, should have been done by government employees.

The Times' analysis showed that the "most secret and politically delicate government jobs, like intelligence collection and budget preparation, are increasingly contracted out, despite regulations forbidding the outsourcing of 'inherently governmental' work ..."

It's been an old canard by the right that government is incompetent. Government bureaucrats can't do anything right. They've worked real hard to make this the conventional wisdom. Big Government is bad. Small Government is good. "Tax and Spend" Democrats want big government, so the cliché goes. They support entitlements like Social Security and Medicare and other social programs that benefit the people.

But, the right and far right favor small government. Privatize as much as you can and get the profits into the hands of private enterprise, has been the battle-cry of the Republicans. Fight entitlements and support discretionary spending—only that which has been voted by Congress. Up military budgets and spending for national security. That's always popular. It's an old ploy. This new outsourcing mania certainly fuels the belief that capitalism has nowhere to go. The spectre of socialism hangs over "the system". In all probability its origin stems back to the fear of the Bolsheviks in the days of Palmer raids after World War I or to the Red Scare pitched by Senator Joseph McCarthy after World War II, or maybe back to the Alien and Sedition Acts of 1798.

The Bush Administration has made it abundantly clear it's at a stalemate.

They can't even win a good, old-fashioned imperialist war against a third-rate nation. The only reasons for the war that can be discerned is to benefit the large corporations that service it; the Halliburtons, the Bechtels, and a myriad of other companies, large and small, that reap their rewards from participating in our national security. These corporations have some clout, too. We know of Vice President Dick Chaney's connection to Halliburton. As for Bechtel, in 1980, Ronald Reagan's presidential campaign was run by George Shultz, president of Bechtel. Casper Weinberger was vice president and general council of Bechtel. Shultz was appointed Secretary of State and Weinberger, Secretary of Defense in the Reagan Administration. It's a good example of how corporate power and government have been intertwined. One learned gentleman, who should know, Benito Mussolini, pre-World War II Italian dictator, who coined the word "fascism" said it should be called "corporatism"—the combined power of corporations and government.

George W. Bush has brought the concept of outsourcing to the military. In Iraq, apparently, he couldn't count on the US Army to do the job so he contracted part of it out to a private company, Blackwater, a private military and security firm. The company describes itself as a "military, law enforcement, security, peacekeeping, and stability operations company". In other words, "mercenaries". With all of this, they still haven't been able to defeat the insurgents "who swim among the people like fish in water" as one Vietnamese described the process.

Bush's answer to defeat in Iraq is to start another war, the target, of course, Iran. He has two rationales that are working for him, Iran's nuclear program and, as Bush charges quite frequently, Iran's "meddling" in Iraq by helping out fellow Shiites. Meddling? (Look who's calling the kettle black)

The drumbeats have begun. And the mainstream media is picking up the rhythm. The usual prognosticators say the attack will come in April.

America, Beware! Iran is not Iraq. Ahmadinejad is not the patsy the Shah was. Remember the hostage crisis of 1979 when 66 Americans were held in Iran for three months during the Iranian Islamic Revolution? As the saying goes, "Don't Mess with Texas!" The same can be said of Teheran.

An attack on Iran would be catastrophic for America. The Shiite government of Iran and its army of close to one million would immediately go to the aid of the Shia in Iraq. That undoubtedly would lead to "helicopter from Embassy roof evacuation time".

Iran could use its missiles, courtesy of China and Russia, to hit our troops in Iraq and our carrier fleets already assembled in the Persian Gulf.

Syria could contribute its large stocks of chemical and biological weapons.

The flow of oil through the Strait of Hormuz could be cut off. Between 15 and 16.5 million barrels of oil transit the Strait each day, roughly 20 percent of the world's daily oil production. How would you like paying ten bucks a gallon for gasoline?

The US government would undoubtedly declare martial law and use anti-terrorist laws and military force against Americans who protest, predicts Eric Herter, former APTN producer.

And that's only for starters. If Israel is hit, you can anticipate a nuclear response and that could be curtains for this planet.

You won't have to wait for the outcome of Global Warming.

Loyal Opposition

In the beginning, there was the word. Two words. Magna Carta.

It was less a document than a series of concessions wrung from the English King John by his rebellious barons in 1215 AD; for the first time, putting a limit on the power of kings. The democrats had their victory.

Seven hundred and ninety-two years later, in 2007 AD, the Democrats are not doing as well against King George. Democratic Majority Leader, Nancy Pelosi, hooked some clauses about setting a timeline for getting out of Iraq onto a funding bill for the war. The rebellious barons in Congress are having a tougher time trying to reign in the power of the king because they're a little timid about what to do. King George accused them of "not supporting our troops" by interfering with his war. Looks like George is going to veto the bill and we'll all be back to square one. Now what's a rebellious baron to do? To fund or not to fund …? That is the question.

The mother country also handed down a bit of democratic software from ages past—"the Loyal Opposition"—the concept that one can be opposed to the actions of the government or ruling party without being opposed to the constitution of the political system. It's a handy concept in wartime, because then, one party, "the loyal opposition" can be critical of the other party's handling of the war without having to worry about "not supporting the troops". The rebellious barons in Congress don't seem to have grasped that concept, yet.

While their base is clamoring at the gate and practically tearing down the walls to protect their civil and human rights under King George, the barons dither. In 2006, the electorate told the Democrats, loud and clear, they want an end to this war and a restoration of the civil rights that had been torn away from them in the euphonious "war on terror". But they are fearful. They should replay Franklin D. Roosevelt's words, "We have nothing to fear, but fear itself." Dave Letterman replays those words, again and again, almost every night.

A gift of democratic hardware handed down with the mother lode was "Habeas Corpus". Now there's a piece of work that has some clout.

The literal meaning of the term is: "you're holding a body". The writ commands the person (or governmental authority) holding the body to bring it into court and show cause as to why it shouldn't be let go.

Right now, the US government is "holding" four or five or six hundred bodies in prison camps on the southern tip of Cuba. (What the hell is a piece of the United States doing down there, anyway?) These bodies have been labeled "enemy combatants" by King George in an ephemeral terrorist war and so, according to him, they are exempt from Habeas Corpus.

Nowhere! Nowhere in the Magna Carta does it say that "enemy combatants" are exempt from Habeas Corpus! But I don't see those writs flying down to Guantanamo Bay. What's happened to the rebellious barons in the Congress? Fear again. Fear of the little shrub. Our British antecedents must be struck dumb with wonder.

Of course, there is one caveat. There's a presidential election coming up and some of those Congressional barons have thrown their hats into the ring, or has that express become as obsolete as "writ of Habeas Corpus"?

You must remember, it's a very sensitive time. Presidential candidates must be very careful they don't say or do the wrong thing during this period of winnowing money and covering all bets, especially if one is the wife of an ex-President and another overly clean. Twenty-six million. Twenty-five million. That's a lot of moolah! And that's only for the primary. With dineros like that, surely, he or she must be in somebody's pocket.

One bad slip on a banana peel and you've had it. McCain took one when he showed how safe it was to walk the streets in a Baghdad market in full armor and talk about how we were winning the war.

But there is one thing the Democrats can do with impunity. Play "the Loyal Opposition" card. We haven't really had a loyal opposition in this country for a long time and it would surely go over with the voters.

Take the raging bull by the horns and opportunity by the forelock. The Iraq war is the chippie. The Middle East is burning.

Our service men and women are running in circles looking for terrorists, knocking down doors, terrorizing Iraqis, killing civilians, and in the process becoming terrorists, themselves. The rate of death among our own servicemen continues to mount, eight last week, sixty-seven last month. How long are we going to let this outrage go on? Will somebody please find the outrage? Where has it gone?

Whichever presidential candidate has the fortitude to step forward and say, "here is the outrage, let's end it now," will become the next president of the United States.

Little Boy and Fat Man

"Little Boy" and "Fat Man" were the names given to the first two nuclear weapons ever dropped on civilian populations. Japan was the target. It happened toward the end of World War II.

Little Boy was dropped on Hiroshima from a B-29 bomber, piloted by US Army Air Force Col. Paul W. Tibbets, who named his plane "Enola Gay" in honor of his mother, the night before the atomic attack.

Fat Man, was a more complicated and powerful plutonium weapon with a force equal to 20 kilotons of TNT devastating more that two square miles of Nagasaki and caused approximately 45,000 immediate deaths..

The wallop that hit Hiroshima and Nagasaki on August 6th and August 9th, 1945, ended the war that was already about to end and left a metallic taste in everybody's mouth. These unnecessary and militarily useless acts, falsely postulating it would end the war sooner, has caused the United States a legacy of shame.

History has a way of reincarnating itself as well as repeating itself.

Do we have, today, a reincarnation of Little Boy, a small nation in the Middle East, alleged to have an arsenal of 200 or more nuclear weapons, threatening and attacking its neighbors?

And do we have a Fat Man, massively endowed with nuclear weapons, in a special relationship with Little Boy, who goes about threatening and attacking smaller and weaker nations?

Daniel Pipes, American historian and counter terrorism analyst who specializes in the Middle East, had this to say about it: "... by special relationship they mean that relations between the two countries have over the last half century blossomed not just into a thick forest of diplomatic and military links, but also into a unique range of economic, academic, religious and personal bonds. From a comparative perspective, the United

States and Israel may well be the most extraordinary tie in international politics."

Mearsheimer and Walt, University professors, who stirred a controversy with their joint article called "The Israel Lobby", published in the London Review of Books, put it this way: "The combination of unwavering support for Israel and the related effort to spread 'democracy' throughout the region has inflamed Arab and Islamic opinion and jeopardized not only US security but that of much of the rest of the world. This situation has no equal in American political history ... Israel has been the largest annual recipient of direct economic and military assistance since 1976 ... and since World War II, to the tune of well over $140 billion (in 2004 dollars)."

We all know about the "special relationship" between the United States and Israel and we all know of America's zealous support of "Israel's right to defend itself."

We have all heard President George W. Bush exclaim, repeatedly, that he would not stand for any Middle East nation having a nuclear weapon—except, apparently, for Israel's alleged 200 or more nuclear weapons in its arsenal.

Bush went to war with Iraq in March of 2003 because of its alleged weapons of mass destruction which turned out to be non-existent. (Other reasons were devised later.)

Bush is now threatening Iran because it has a nuclear program and is enriching uranium; for nuclear power, the Iranians say, but it's not a stretch to believe they will go for a weapon, just as North Korea did when it was threatened by Fat Boy.

The Nuclear Non-Proliferation Treaty (NPT or NNPT) was signed by 189 nations beginning in 1981 for the purpose of limiting the spread of nuclear weapons. The eight confirmed nuclear powers (those who have openly tested nuclear weapons) and the one presumed nuclear power (Israel) have neither signed nor ratified the treaty.

Most signers claim that Article VI of the treaty constitutes a formal and specific obligation on the part of the major nuclear powers to disarm themselves of nuclear weapons and have decried the fact they have failed to do so.

The last time the "big two", the US and Russia, even tried to cut down on the number of warheads each had, the effort ended in failure. A treaty signed in Moscow with great fanfare by President George W. Bush and President Vladimir Putin, in May of 2002, called on both sides to reduce their strategic nuclear warheads to between 1,700 and 2,200 by the year 2012.

It hasn't happened yet and it doesn't look as though it ever will. US Undersecretary of Energy Linton Brooks told a Senate Subcommittee that the retained warheads will be needed for routine maintenance of the arsenal, for meeting "commitments to allies," and to address threats that may arise in the future. Was he thinking of the attack on Iraq in 2003?

The current US nuclear arsenal is estimated by experts to contain between 6,500 and 7,000 weapons.

Would Fat Boy think of going to war to stop Ahmadinejad from getting the bomb?

"It is too late to stop the progress of Iran," Ahmadinejad told reporters at a defiant news conference. "We have broken through to a new stage and it is too late to push us back."

Ahmadinejad also warned the UN Security Council, telling the world body not to risk playing with a "lion's tail". "They say that Iran is a lion sat down in a corner. And we tell them: Do not play with the lion's tail."

Maybe a lion's tail can break a Fat Boy. Remember, he's in a corner and he has the right to defend himself. So says the United Nations Charter.

So don't be too hard on Ahmadinejad of Iran. He may be looking for a deterrent weapon as he sees Little Boy and Fat Man coming at him.

George Bush Proves the Rule

Isaac Newton's Third Law of Motion, formulated in the 17th Century says, "For every action, there is an equal and opposite reaction." Why would George W. Bush, in the 21st Century, set out to prove the rule?

Since 9/11, the President has demonized Arab terrorists, now he's giving operating control of our major east coast ports to a company owned by the Arab state of Dubai, reputed supporter of the Taliban and Arab terrorists. Is that an equal, or opposite reaction?

But this is only the top of the cracker barrel. The corporate oligarchy that runs America has been selling it off for decades with GATT, WTO, NAFTA and other acronyms that spell free trade, globalization and a flat world. We're now scraping the bottom of the barrel. The Dubai Port World deal is just the latest idiocy.

Doesn't this nation of ours, the greatest country in the world, have the ingenuity, the entrepreneurial know-how and the skilled and unskilled labor to run our own ports? Do we have to outsource everything?

Think for a minute.

It's the multi-national corporate world, stupid.

Nationalism is becoming obsolete. The nation state, with all its narcissism, hoopla and pride in achievement, is fast disappearing. The fading glory is reflected in the fading enthusiasm of the recent Olympic games where nationalism was once the most exciting feature of the event.

The United States of America is well on its way to being hollowed out. Before we know it, we'll be a highly militarized state with some low-paying service jobs. Even our armaments will be manufactured abroad.

Take auto, for example. We had an automobile industry that was the envy of the world—and we had the hard-fought and hard-won Auto Workers Union that gave assembly line workers wages of $24 an hour and more and a bridge into the middle class. These were people with purchasing power, who could buy the things they made. Today, it's a race to the bottom. Means of production are moved to the places where wages are lowest. That's flattening the world.

We had labor leaders like John L. Lewis and Walter Reuther who set an example for workers in basic industry—steel, mining, electrical, communications. Even the teamsters, under the leadership of Dan Tobin and Jimmy Hoffa, had one of the highest standards of living of any union in America.

Today, the unions may still be there, but where have all the workers gone?

Ford eliminated 35,000 jobs and five plants in the last five years and has just announcement that it was eliminating nearly 30,000 blue collar and 4,000 white-collar jobs and 12 percent of its officers by 2012. General Motors announced it would close 12 plants and lay off 30,000. Chrysler, bought by German automaker Daimler, announced that it will eliminate 6,000 white-collar jobs in the near future. What used to be known as the Big Three automakers have cut 140,000 jobs—one-third of their North American work force—since the year 2000.

There are now three major foreign automakers in America—Toyota, Honda and Nissan—overshadowing the original American big three. The current issue of Consumer Reports doesn't even include the product of an American auto company in its list of the top ten safest cars.

This is just for starters.

Thom Hartmann, author of *What would Jefferson Do?* and *Ultimate Sacrifice,* says that "foreign companies are buying up our water systems, our power generating systems, our mines, and our few remaining factories. All because 'flat world' so-called 'free trade' policies have turned us from a nation of wealthy producers into a nation of indebted consumers, leaving the world awash in dollars that are most easily used to buy off big chunks of America."

According to US Government statistics, 97% of our sound recording industries is foreign owned, 65% of metal ore mining, 63% of book publishers, 62% of cement, concrete, lime and gypsum products, 53% of the rubber industry, and on and on....

Now, Bush notices that America is addicted to oil. We've been hooked for a long time and there's nothing much we can do about it. Alternative energy sources have been around for a long time but the oil giants have had us by the throat. They're not going to let go easily. They've got the President and the Vice President to wield their big sticks to protect oil. Bush would rather fight the world for the last drop of oil than start a crash program for developing large scale alternative energy.

George W. Bush now thinks he's the United Nations. He goes to India and makes nuclear deals that only an international organization (the United Nations) and the International Atomic Energy Agency (IAEA) should make. In his inimitable way, he has set off a new wave of consternation over proliferation. I don't blame the smaller countries for trying to get a nuclear deterrent. They see what's happened to Afghanistan and Iraq.

If Bush is thinking of solving the energy problem with nuclear power, we're back to square one—when Three Mile Island blew. With the Chinese government announcing that it plans to build as many as 30 new nuclear reactors by the year 2020, the world is in real trouble. When this sinks in, it will put Iran and North Korea on a back burner. It makes the US, Russia and China the main proliferations.

Perhaps if the great powers started abiding by the Nuclear Non Proliferation Treaty (NPT) they all signed, and began destroying the thousands of nuclear weapons they each have stockpiled, as they promised they would do, we might get somewhere.

For every action, there is an equal and opposite reaction.

The Whole Truth and Nothing But ...

As a writer of a memoir, I better get my licks in this raging bruh-ha-ha over James Frey's bestseller "A Million Little Pieces" before it blows over, which it surely will in a few days.

Frey has been getting unshirted hell, from every direction, ever since a website bombed his book alleging factual error in his memoir. The Oprah Winfrey-backed book, nevertheless, has sold three and a half million copies so far, and counting.

The big question is: is it cricket to have fictional segments in a memoir? As President Clinton might say, that depends on what the definition of memoir is.

I defined my book as an "unauthorized" memoir because I wrote it against my better judgment, an oxymoron to begin with. It's about my thirty years working in Network News while being a card-carrying member of the Communist Party. Wow! Who said the news media had a liberal bias?

There are two errors of fact right in that last paragraph. The Communist Party disintegrated out from under me in 1955, two years after I got the job at CBS News as writer and story editor. The second error of fact is that there was no such thing as a "card-carrying member" because the Communist Party didn't issue cards, during that clandestine period at the height of the McCarthy era.

They say—"they" being some amorphous group of experts—that a memoir doesn't have to be truthful or factual because it's the writer's vision, a subjective view of his or her life that's being told. The writer may imagine things that didn't happen. Does that make sense?

Who would want to read a pack of lies?

A reader of a novel would, even if the book is made up out of whole cloth, as long as it tells a good story. That's called "creative fiction". But Frey's book isn't a novel.

James Frey claims his book is "creative non-fiction"—a memoir. A memoir, traditionally, has less defined rules. This one, not only tells a good story of addiction and redemption in Frey's life, but also includes a few incidents that he made up. The book resonated with millions of readers who got caught up in it and many say reading it was life altering. That's the mark of a good writer. Readers felt the honesty of the work. Frey claims that only about 5% of his story is fabricated. If you can produce that kind of an effect with words, why tinker with it? Or is that like being a little bit pregnant?

All this noodling takes us back to the concept of "absolute truth". Does it exist? Some religious people and some ideologues believe it does. I've always been taught there is no such thing as absolute truth. Truth can only be relative. It's been that way ever since Adam and Eve ate the apple from the Tree of Knowledge. Why change now?

The climate of truth in a society or in a country is palpable. When deception and dissembling become the order of the day, people can lose their sensitivity to the truth. That's why propaganda is so effective at times of decision and at times of crisis. People can normally sniff out the falsehoods in a book or in a situation. But at times of apathy, they tend to let it glide by and lies become accepted as truth.

Determining truth is something everyone has to divine for his or her self. I've been a journalist all my life. The one absolute for me (I won't say truth) is that in writing, in any medium, your **facts** have to be right. You can interpret those facts in different ways. Therein lies the rub.

An editor said to me once, in great anger, because he didn't like the story I submitted, "Your facts are right, I just don't like the facts you used!" That didn't cut much ice with an honest editorial board. I suppose, I, or another writer, could go out on the same story and get another set of facts that could be interpreted in another way to satisfy that editor.

We're witnessing a lot of hanky-panky with the facts in the Bush administration. They tell one lie after another to the American people and the world. Many of their most outrageous lies are linked to foreign policy and the war in Iraq. They admit to bad intelligence and they use this as an excuse to manufacture the facts to fit the policy. This was exposed in the infamous Downing Street memos. The climate of truth in America today is in the greenhouse.

In a stroll down memory lane, in journalism and publishing, history and politics, the road is littered with fakes, fabricators and plagiarists. Some are washed up, some are functioning nicely. It's not surprising. It's something that's been going on for a long time. As long as there have been writers, there have been some with super imaginations. It doesn't necessarily make them inferior writers. It just makes some of them liars.

Confounding the Founding Fathers

Our Founding Fathers would surely be confounded today by the way the democratic system upon which they founded this country is running out of steam.

Adapted from the British attempt at democracy, starting with the Magna Carta, ours began as a democracy in the narrowest sense of the word; a democracy for the ruling class. The vote was restricted to white, male, landed gentry. But the Founding Fathers devised a system of checks and balances, three branches of government—executive, legislative, judiciary—splitting the responsibilities of power to keep each other honest. Thomas Jefferson inserted the Bill of Rights, the first ten amendments to the Constitution and turned it into a work of art.

Around the same time, the late 1700s, Britain's Industrial Revolution was booming along, making its way across the Atlantic. Entrepreneurs were looking for raw materials and markets. The new manufacturing class that sprang up to meet the need, fit right in with the landed gentry.

But that was then. This is now. What we have today is a maze of interlocking directorates, intertwined corporate oligarchies, each out to seize the wealth, the power and control of government. The executive branch has become a brazen, authoritarian bungle, the legislative has invalidated itself and the judiciary has become the flunky of the executive branch.

Cindy Sheehan put it boldly in her farewell letter to America, "if we don't find alternatives to this corrupt "two" party system our Representative Republic will die and be replaced with what we are rapidly descending into with nary a check or balance: a fascist corporate wasteland."

If the media, once called "the press", and our elected representatives in Congress, began paying some attention to the present state of affairs, we might not, now, be on the edge of an abyss.

You don't have to go far, or to any great lengths, to learn the truth. Even the New York Times, our paper of record, brings you some of it, sometimes even on page one, albeit below the fold.

A case in point: the report of the Clintons, Hillary and Bill, and their benefactor, Vinod Gupta, in the New York Times (5–26–07). The Times describes a $146,000 vacation trip that Gupta and his company, infoUSA, one of the nation's largest brokers of information on consumers, provided for the Clintons. The company also paid more than $2 million dollars for consultant services to Bill and almost $900,000 "to fly him around the world for his presidential foundation work and to fly Mrs. Clinton to campaign events".

All this came to light because shareholders of infoUSA sued Mr. Gupta for wasting the company's money trying "to ingratiate himself" with his high profile guests.

Perhaps the story has been effectively squelched because it doesn't seem to have sprouted wings. However, the presidential campaign has a long way to go, and we may be hearing a lot more about Hillary's corporate connections when the dirt starts flying.

There's nothing unusual about corporate pandering to politicians and vice versa. In one form or another it's a pretty common occurrence. It happens all the time.

The Washington Post rapped Tom DeLay, (R-Tex), formerly House Majority Whip, by reporting a trip he made to London and Scotland, the air fare charged to an American Express credit card issued to Jack Abramoff, the Washington lobbyist, now convicted of federal crimes and spending time in the slammer. Abramoff also provided gifts and political donations to DeLay in exchange for favors to Abramoff's lobbying clients, which included the Northern Mariana Islands, Internet gambling services, and several Native American tribes with gambling interests.

It all has to do with money and power. Electoral corruption goes back to those original landed gentry who devised this nation. In 1777, James

Madison lost a race for the Virginia legislature, which he claimed was due to his refusal to provide alcohol to some of his constituents. Some politicians had been known to buy votes and pay a premium for repeat voters. In 1823, the price of a vote in New York City was $5 and for repeat voters it went as high as $30. New York Senator Hillary Rodham Clinton paid her chief strategist, Mark Penn, $1 million for her re-election campaign in '06 and $277,000 in the first quarter of this year, according to The Nation Magazine. That's not too far out of line considering the inflation rate since 1823.

Corporate America likes to have our politicians safely in their pockets.

Campaign Finance Reform was supposed to correct all this. Remember McCain-Feingold?

Yes, they sponsored the bill that passed into law as the Bipartisan Campaign Reform Act (BCRA) of 2002. The law prohibited unregulated contributions (called "soft money") to national political parties. No more contributions in the hundreds of thousands of dollars by the high rollers to their favored political party were allowed.

Did that stop 'em? No way. Every loop has its technology readily accepted by Congress. So corporations were still able to buy their politician of choice. Lobbyists still performed the K Street waltz, and the PACs continued to proliferate. The NRA and AIPAC and AARP and ACLU, et al, were still able to do their thing. The special interests still have their way and the average Joe is still left out in the cold.

There was a time when the acronyms were different—when the NRA meant National Recovery Act. There was the CCC and the AAA, the WPA, the NLRB and the TVA, and more, that grew out of Roosevelt's New Deal. They were designed to help people.

"We, the people …" had a stake in our country and in our government. The unions, and the minorities, had their place under the big tent of the Democratic Party.

Our Founding Fathers would have recognized us then, but if they could see America today, our Founding Fathers would certainly be confounded.

PART II
Left Hooks

James R. Hoffa—Lessons Learned

The perennial hunt for the remains of Jimmy Hoffa, former Teamster chief, is on again. The FBI is now digging up a farm in Michigan not far from where Jimmy was last seen, at the Machus Red Fox Restaurant in Bloomfield, Michigan on July 30, 1975. He was allegedly meeting there with a couple of Mafia capos. Never found, he was declared legally dead in 1983.

Why has this interest in Jimmy Hoffa persisted even after 30 years? Is there something about this charismatic labor leader people still want to know? A look back might provide the answer. In 1974, a year before his disappearance, I produced an investigative biography called *Closeup: Hoffa* for ABC News.

Hoffa began the fight to get his job back with the Teamsters, when he was released from prison in 1971. The early '70s was a volatile time. The Vietnam War was grinding to an end and Nixon was working his way toward a resignation. Hoffa's fight to retake leadership of the Teamsters was a story of high drama that gave us a way a different window from which to look into the labor movement in America.

For all its history, the assault on labor has been overwhelming, continuous, inhuman and destructive from the beginning of the industrial revolution to this very day. No wonder unions are dysfunctional and chaotic. So are most of their leaders. If they're not coerced, co-opted or corrupted, they're framed, jailed or neutralized in some way. Only when capitalism is in the throes of crisis, deep depression and near collapse can labor leaders like Eugene V. Debs or John L. Lewis emerge.

Debs organized the American Railway Union, an industrial union for all railroad workers in 1893, became a confirmed Socialist while serving time in prison for refusing to comply with a federal court injunction, ran for President of the United States four times on the Socialist Party ticket, the last time from prison in 1920 and received nearly 1 million votes.

John L. Lewis led the United Mine Workers in organizing most of the coal industry, was one of the organizers of the Congress of Industrial Organizations (CIO) in 1936 and joined the Reuther brothers, Walter and Victor, in organizing the United Auto Workers' sit-in strikes against General Motors at their Flint, Michigan plants.

For 44 bitterly cold winter days the auto workers in Flint held out, eventually inspiring more than two-thirds of General Motors 145 thousand other production workers to strike as well, at dozens of other plants. The strikers in Flint seized, shut down and occupied one, then two, and then three of the key GM plants. Suddenly, workers everywhere were sitting-down. There were 477 sit-down strikes by the end of 1937, involving more than half a million workers.

Mighty GM had vowed publicly that it would never allow the UAW to represent its employees. But the General Motors Corporation ended up granting that crucial right—and more—to the union. It was a stunning victory for the United Auto Workers. It led the way—and swiftly—to the unionization of workers throughout heavy industry and, ultimately, to unionization in all fields. It certainly was the high water mark of labor power in America.

How did Jimmy Hoffa stack up along side a Debs or a John L. Lewis?

On the one hand, he had used the rank and file as his personal power base, on the other, he had given them one of the highest standards of living of any union in America. He negotiated the Master Freight Agreement, a national contract with the employers, one of the best in the country, yet he was charged with robbing the members' pension funds. It was this kind of cockeyed contradiction in the man that intrigued me.

When I met Hoffa in the summer of 1974, at sixty-two, he was short, vigorous and feisty. Hair slicked back, graying at the temples, Jimmy had that charisma, the kind they accuse Bill Clinton of having—the kind of charm and "friendmanship" that puts you in the center of his universe. Yet the ingratiating smile covered some shifting of eyes and flashes of anger. It was understandable. He was under enormous pressure—trying to recover his old position in the union.

Hoffa made his fight to regain the Teamster Presidency a personal matter. He said: *I've been in it all my life. It's my life the way I lived it, the way I want to live it …*

A union organizer since he was a teenager, Hoffa grew up with the labor movement in this country. His ideas and tactics were formed in the crucible of violence that was labor's early history. In 1931, at the age of 18, Hoffa organized the loading dock at the Kroger Company's Detroit warehouse.

Hoffa learned early that trade unions in America were forced to fight for survival with bargaining, boycotts and blood. Most of the time, union violence was provoked by industry and government's use of force, exemplified in 1937 when Chicago police killed ten striking steel workers in a bloody, historic battle—the Memorial Day Massacre. Early union organizers risked not only their jobs, but their lives. Hoffa recalled it this way: *If they found out that you even passed out literature or talked union, you were subject to getting your skull broke …*

Like all major unions, the Teamsters were no strangers to violence. In 1934, Teamster Local 544 in Minneapolis went on strike. A look at early Teamster history provides a better understanding of how Hoffa's ideas on the labor struggle were formed. He recalled: *In 1934, they had nothing to lose except the fact they may lose their life and that wasn't worth much at that time because they couldn't do nothing with their life…. And when you listen to a man like Vince or Ray Dunne talk or Farrell Dobbs talk …*

Farrell Dobbs and the Dunne Brothers had been Trotskyites in Minneapolis in the thirties and organizers of Local 544 of the International Brotherhood of Teamsters.

By mentioning Farrell Dobbs, Hoffa opened the door to a deeper probe of his character, permitting him to be more fully judged as a labor leader.

In 1934, Farrell Dobbs led the Minneapolis Teamster strike that resulted in a hostile 10-day armed conflict with police and 3000 National Guard troops.

We wanted to hear Farrell Dobbs talk, as Hoffa suggested … and we did. We tracked Dobbs down, living in retirement, outside Berkeley, California. He was a tall, gaunt man in his seventies, somewhat haggard. A lifetime in the labor struggle must have taken its toll. But his eyes lit up when he talked about the Minneapolis strike of 1934: *We came to battle … the battle focused in the market district in Minneapolis, the wholesale produce market district in Minneapolis. And we fought it out there, club to club … and the result was that we were able to fight the cops to a draw and they had to negotiate a settlement with us.*

One of the outstanding things is not only the courage but the resourcefulness that a body of workers show when they're in a mood to fight and they have leaders that are willing to lead them into a fight.

A look at this history provides a clue to understanding how Hoffa's ideas on the labor struggle were formed. Hoffa says of Dobbs: *Farrell kept preaching the fact that nobody could, in the future, nobody would be able to win in their own town or their own state, but had to have expanded coverage for the entire transportation, warehousing and food industry. I realized how right he was and it had an impact on my mind as to the fact that the union could no longer survive, no matter how well organized, in a particular city or state … without wider coverage.*

Farrell Dobbs explained to us what he did: *In the Midwest, we concentrated on a uniform contract for the whole eleven-state area where we had organized the workers. Hoffa was definitely a member of the leadership team.*

By the end of the 1930's, Dobbs had made the Midwest a Teamster stronghold. Dobbs was responsible for the concept of area-wide bargaining—the idea of getting regional and then national contracts. Years later, Hoffa used Dobbs' ideas in developing the National Master Freight Agreement.

His relationship with Farrell Dobbs was an important chapter in Hoffa's life. Dobbs and the Dunne brothers' political affiliation with the Socialist Workers Party in Minnesota exerted a strong influence on the young Jimmy Hoffa. But Hoffa's friendship with Dobbs reached a turning point in 1941 with the entry of the United States into World War II. The

Socialist Workers Party was against the war. Dobbs and the Dunne brothers organized Teamster opposition to the US entry.

At that time, Dan Tobin was the General President of the International Brotherhood of Teamsters and a close friend of Franklin D. Roosevelt. President Roosevelt did not want Socialists in powerful labor positions during wartime, and he asked his friend Tobin to do something about it.

With war beginning in Europe, Tobin ordered Hoffa to have the International take over Minneapolis Local 544 and get rid of Dobbs and the Dunn brothers.

Although Hoffa's idealism toward the working-class struggle made him respect Dobbs, Hoffa's pragmatism in his fight for power led to his betrayal of Dobbs. Viewed today, this can be interpreted as a turning point in Hoffa's career. Hoffa rationalized his actions this way: *I think that he [Tobin] used our relationship because I had refused to go on a request, or on an order. When he ordered me to go to Minneapolis, I said I wouldn't go and it was none of my business. And then he put it on a personal basis, as a request, and brought up what he had done for me and so forth—and what he was gonna do for me. And once the old man made a request, at his age, you couldn't very well turn him down. Recognizing he was the General President, I went there ... went to Minneapolis, took over the office, brought in a hundred crack guys, had the war. We won every battle. And we finally took the union over and then Farrell left and went with the Socialist Party.*

Farrell Dobbs recalled it differently: *Now it is true that Hoffa was among the IBT goon squads that Tobin sent into Minneapolis against Local 544 in 1941. That's actually true. But Hoffa says, he says that he whipped us. Now, it's a little more complicated than that. Hoffa got just a little help, if he thinks he whipped us. For instance, he was helped by the Minneapolis Police Department, the courts of the city, the county, and the state ... the Mayor, the Governor and an anti-labor law that had been rigged and put through by the Republican Governor of the State—and by the Federal Bureau of Investigation, the United States Department of Justice and Franklin Delano Roosevelt, who then happened to be President of the United States ...*

Under those circumstances, you got to admit Hoffa had just a little help, didn't he? The man exaggerates on this point. He exaggerates.

Hoffa's fast and determined rise to power began—many think—with the betrayal of Farrell Dobbs and the takeover of the rebellious Minneapolis local.

Dave Beck, who was elected General President of the International in 1952, took over a position he could not have achieved without Hoffa's support. But again, Hoffa has been accused of later trying to eliminate Beck by arranging, in 1957, to feed information on Beck to a Senate subcommittee holding hearings on corrupt union practices. Beck was later convicted of grand larceny and tax evasion and spent two and a half years in prison.

With Beck out of the way, Hoffa became General President of the Teamsters in 1957, climaxing a rise to power that would escalate contract benefits for the working teamster and, at the same time, plunge the union into corruption and scandal from which it has not yet recovered. Hoffa held the position of General President of the International for thirteen years, even after he went to prison in 1967.

If Jimmy Hoffa was the end product of the violence and corruption that marked the history of America's labor movement, he was also a symbol of labor's victories and its power. Labor is an arena where corruption and idealism are part of the same tradition.

When John F. Kennedy was elected President in 1960, he appointed his brother Robert as US Attorney General. Bobby had been on Hoffa's tail since he was Chief Counsel of Senator McClellan's committee, in the fifties, investigating crime in the labor movement. Now, Bobby and his brother continued their crusade to get organized crime out of organized labor. Hoffa became their prime target. Of course, organized big business cheered them on.

During the Kennedy Administration, Jimmy Hoffa found himself battling employers, on the one hand, to put through the unique Master Freight Agreement and fighting just as hard, on the other, to stay out of jail.

For Hoffa, the Kennedy years were punctuated by a continuing series of legal battles waged in courtrooms around the country. In the past, Hoffa had usually come out ahead in his brushes with the law. In 1957, he was acquitted on charges of Congressional bribery. Later, he was tried twice for wiretap conspiracy involving alleged spying on Teamster subordinates. The first trial ended in a hung jury. In the second, in 1958, Hoffa was acquitted. Charges of mail and wire fraud brought against Hoffa in 1960 were dropped.

In 1962, the Kennedy Administration brought a case against Hoffa in Nashville, Tennessee. Hoffa was charged with accepting illegal payments from employers. Once more, though, the government failed to make its charges stick. The case ended in a hung jury, split 7 to 5 in Hoffa's favor. But the stormy Nashville trial contained the seeds of further trouble for Jimmy Hoffa.

The government kept Hoffa and his associates under close surveillance throughout the Nashville trial. One Hoffa aide, Edward Grady Partin, was secretly acting as a government informer. The result was evidence that led to Hoffa's subsequent indictment on charges of tampering with the jury in an effort to fix the verdict in the Nashville trial.

This jury tampering case was tried in Chattanooga in 1964. Throughout the six-week trial, Hoffa and his attorneys complained bitterly about the government's tactics.

But the jury found Hoffa guilty and he was sentenced to eight years in Federal prison. It was a stunning setback for Jimmy and he protested vigorously that his conviction was unjust.

Within weeks after his Chattanooga conviction, Hoffa was back in court, again, this time in Chicago. He was charged with fraud in connection with as elaborate scheme to swindle money from the Union's Pension Fund.

Again, Hoffa was convicted. The judge added another five years imprisonment to the eight years Hoffa got at the Chattanooga trial. On March 7, 1967, Hoffa was sent to the Federal penitentiary in Lewisburg, Pennsylvania. The Kennedy Justice department had gotten its man!

Supreme Court Chief Justice Earl Warren called Hoffa's conviction "an affront to the quality and fairness of Federal law enforcement."

James Neal, the federal prosecutor in the Chattanooga trial who succeeded in nailing Hoffa said later: *In the last ten years, as I've gotten a little older, and hopefully a little wiser, I have some discomfort with the thought that if the Federal government pursues any man long enough and hard enough, it's very difficult for him to escape.*

Hoffa refused to give up the Presidency of the union, appointing Frank Fitzsimmons, his General Vice-president, as caretaker. During the next four years, Hoffa had three parole hearings, all of which were rejected, partially because of his refusal to give up the Presidency. Finally, in June of 1971, Hoffa announced his retirement from the union—and, at about the same time, Fitzsimmons won election to the Presidency. This cleared the way for Fitzsimmons to take office. It also set the stage for Jimmy's release from prison.

President Richard Nixon commuted Hoffa's sentence on December 23, 1971, and Hoffa left prison the same day.

Even though government administrations had changed, Democrats were out, Republicans and Nixon were in—and Hoffa had served his prison term, he was not yet a free man.

Hoffa had appealed the restriction on his commutation that barred him from union activity until 1980, and was awaiting Federal Court action. Hoffa claims that when he walked out of Lewisburg Penitentiary on December 23rd of 1971, he did not know about the restriction.

Hoffa explains it this way: *I found out about the restriction from a reporter we met at the airport. The prison didn't release news of the restriction to the press until four fourteen in the afternoon. I had been released at four o'clock. They knew that once I was outside of the gate, there was nothing I could do about the restriction. They were fearful that I would not accept the commutation if I knew that restriction was in there. I certainly would not have! I would have been out of prison in 1974 without restriction.*

To check out Hoffa's story, we went to the Federal Bureau of Prisons archives and dug up some documents.

Document 1: Conditions of Parole, with no mention of a restriction, signed by James Riddle Hoffa on <u>December 22, 1971</u>.

Document 2: Restriction—addendum to commutation dated <u>December 23, 1971.</u>

Hoffa was telling the truth.

Still, in Federal Court, Hoffa was unable to get rid of the restriction and immediately appealed to a higher court.

While Hoffa's fight continued to get the restriction off—the debate raged as to how the restriction got on.

The cast of characters in the controversy is drawn from former President Nixon's white House staff. The three apparent principals were all later involved in the Watergate scandal.

Some Hoffa partisans believe Charles Colson, once Special Counsel to President Nixon engineered the restriction. Colson left the White House for private law practice and immediately Teamster President Frank Fitzsimmons hired his firm. Hoffa remained convinced that Colson had a hand in it: *I'm positively sure that Colson had a hand in it, and I'm positively sure that he was the architect of the language. And Colson did it to ingratiate himself with Fitzsimmons. And in doing so, he got the job of representing the Teamsters. And Fitz did it, through Colson, to be able to keep the presidency of the International Union.*

Frank Fitzsimmons, of course, denies Hoffa's allegations: *There is no truth whatsoever. And as far as Jimmy Hoffa is concerned when he makes that statement, he knows that he's a damned liar. He accuses Chuck Colson and me of creating them restrictions. I didn't know nothing about them restrictions, didn't know anything about 'em until I read it in the newspapers.*

Charles Colson spoke about the Hoffa restriction with us when we got to him two days before he, Colson, went to prison for Watergate related offenses. He spur the following: *The accusation has been made that Fitzsimmons and I cooked this up, some conspiracy, to keep Hoffa from coming back into the Teamsters. That's just plain malarkey ... Fitzsimmons and I never discussed the restrictions on Hoffa's commutation. I advised Mr. Fitzsimmons, I think the day before Hoffa was to be released that he was going to be released under conditions that seemed to be in the best interest of the labor movement and the country at the time. I never told him what, what those restrictions were.*

William Carlos Moore, former head of DRIVE—the Teamsters' political arm—said that he heard Fitzsimmons on the phone with Colson planning the restriction. Moore signed a sworn affidavit to that effect in US District Court.

<u>Document</u>: "Mr. Fitzsimmons … made an observation in substantially the following words: 'Chuck, Hoffa should be released from prison but I think it awfully important that a condition be placed on him that he not be free to seek office and to participate in the labor movement until after he has served his full sentence'."

William Carlos Moore further stated to us: *It became a kind of a standing rule with the administration, I'm talking about the Fitzsimmons administration, that let's get Hoffa out of jail, let's get the Hoffa people off our back, but let's restrict him so he cannot come back into the labor movement.*

What can you learn from probing the life of Jimmy Hoffa?

Certainly Hoffa was not a great labor leader. He might have been a great <u>union</u> leader, for a while. There is a difference. A union leader is pragmatic, working hard to get the best wages and working conditions for his membership. In my view, a true leader in the labor movement has a vision that transcends personal opportunism—a sense of the class struggle in all its ramifications—leaders like Eugene Debs and John L. Lewis.

Hoffa lost it early in his career—at the time of his betray of Farrell Dobbs in 1941, or before. When he agreed to go to Minneapolis with a gang of goons and take over Local 544 ousting Farrell Dobbs and the Dune Brothers, he morally accepted the immorality of the establishment. What did Hoffa say …? *I was just taking orders …*

Where have we heard that before?

Jimmy Hoffa betrayed his friend and mentor. Where do you go from there? Down the slippery slope. Before long, he was robbing his union members of their pension funds.

Yes, Hoffa was pursued relentlessly by prosecutorial hound dogs, as James Neal, Hoffa's prosecutor admitted. That could make any leader obsessive and push him over the edge. Maybe that's what it did to Jimmy.

Everybody asks the question—was Hoffa a gangster? If you have to ask it, the answer is, yes. Well, you can say, he adopted the mores of the employers in using hoodlums and gangsters to attain his ends. Not good enough.

Hoffa never had a snowball's chance of regaining the Presidency of the IBT. The mob was quite satisfied with the pliant Frank Fitzsimmons.

To appease the pro-Hoffa faction in the membership, they got Hoffa released from prison. They didn't expect him to fight that hard to get his job back.

Jimmy should have retired and spent his winters in Florida and summers up "at the lake", as he said he could. Instead, he made a nuisance of himself.

The boys took care of that.

So long, Jimmy. It was good to know ya' …

The Great Deception

The cultivation of the coca plant is not illegal in Colombia.

The criminality begins with the process of making the paste from which refined cocaine hydrochloride powder is extracted after treatment with a variety of chemicals. This process takes place in the cocaine laboratories of the narco-traffickers in all parts of Colombia.

The government, however, fails to make these legal distinctions. It has been waging war against the *campesinos*, the small farmers who grow the coca crop on their little plots of land.

That was one of the facts I learned as a member of the Colombian Support Network delegation to Bogotá and Putumayo on a fact-finding mission, July 8–15, 2001.

We wanted to find out, first hand, what the US-sponsored campaign of herbicide aerial spraying of the coca crop was doing, if anything, to the land and the people of the region, besides killing the coca. The spraying (called "fumigation" in Colombia) is a part of the billion and a half dollar program called "Plan Colombia" devised by the US to fight the "War on Drugs". The stated purpose: to reduce the amount of cocaine flowing into the United States. It may also have another purpose. Eighty percent of the money would go to beefing up Colombia's military, aiding it in its war against the insurgent guerrilla movements, the FARC and the ELN.

Twenty percent of the money would be used for social programs.

In the southern province of Putumayo, where the heaviest concentration of coca is grown and where the FARC is strong, we interviewed dozens of *campesinos* and *campesino* leaders. Part of the 20% of "Plan Colombia" money is used to implement "social pacts" made with the coca-growing *campesinos* in the Putumayo. About half of these have signed the social pacts.

As explained to us by Manuel Alzate Restrepo, the Mayor of Puerto Asis, the largest port on the Putumayo River, these pacts require the *campesino* to voluntarily eradicate his coca crop in return for agricultural assistance, training, technology and monetary resources to successfully raise alternative crops like, yucca, corn, rice and poultry.

The *campesinos* that we spoke with say the government has not lived up to its part of the agreement. What was promised was not delivered. They feel the plan was ill conceived. One of them told us:

> *Who are the ones who are dying in this war? Who are the ones who are accused by both sides of belonging to the other? Who has to walk through these jungles trying to make a living while fearing for his dear life? The campesino.*

The campesinos are angry. They feel they've been blackmailed into signing these pacts. They've been threatened with fumigation if their plots of coca have not been eradicated by year's end. Furthermore, the substitute crops they have been asked to grow do not thrive in the thin soil of this region, adjacent to the rain forests of the Amazon. They will have lost their cash crop, coca, and would be saddled with poor crops that cannot even be gotten to market. They'd be left without a cash crop and no viable means of livelihood.

In Bogotá, we talked with Colombian government officials, academics and experts in the ecology of the land, as well as with the US Ambassador, Anne Patterson, at the US Embassy.

We tried to impart to the Ambassador the sense of fear and anger we observed in the *campesinos* and the people of Putumayo. They are taking the brunt of the "war on drugs".

Colombia is caught in a cruel contradiction—the victim of its horticulture, the coca plant, and history—entangled in a long, drawn-out civil war—the war against the FARC, the principal guerrilla group in the country.

The current crisis is over the fumigation of the coca crop with the Monsanto Chemical Company's herbicide, glyphosate (brand name,

"Roundup" and "Roundup Plus", an ingredient called "Cosmoflux" added).

Supposedly, "Roundup" is a harmless herbicide used against weeds in gardens around the United States. But coca is a stubborn plant and resists glyphosate unless made more toxic by the "Plus" in "Roundup Plus." There is testimony to the effect that the more toxic glyphosate has caused lesions and other ill effects in children and adults caught in the spray of "Roundup Plus".

At our meeting with Ambassador Patterson, one of our delegation members pushed a one-page flyer across the table to her. The flyer was put out in Spanish by the US Department of State telling the people of Putumayo that "Roundup" was perfectly harmless to one's health. There was no mention of "Roundup Plus".

"Wasn't this a deception on the part of the US government?" I asked.

The question wasn't answered but an extensive dialogue ensued about the relative toxicity of the various chemicals involved. Scientific findings were presented. Dueling scientists had divergent opinions on the subject. It brought to mind the debate that raged over the use of Agent Orange in Vietnam. I was tempted, but refrained from asking, "What right does the United States government have, in the first place, to spray herbicides, toxic or otherwise, on the land and people of other countries?"

I knew what the answer would be. "We were invited in to do so by the Colombian government".

The Ambassador made it clear that US drug policy aimed to reduce the amount of cocaine smuggled into the US by cutting down the amount of coca leaves grown.

Dr. Hairo Lara, an ecological economist at a Bogotá University, explained to us that this thinking was a gross irrationality.

Coca plants are not immune from the economic laws of supply and demand. If the supply of coca leaves goes down, the price goes up. Enterprising entrepreneurs rush into the market, disperse and grow more coca to take advantage of the higher price. This has been the experience of coca spraying for the past twenty-five years when *tebuthiuron* was the defoliant of choice for coca plant eradication. Today, there is more coca in more places than ever before.

Dr. Ricardo Vargas, of Andean Action (Acción Andina), an environmental organization that specializes in analyzing the fumigations told us:

> *The amount of narco-trafficking does not depend on the amount of coca grown. On the contrary, the amount of coca grown is determined by the amount of narco-trafficking. In 1997, 50% of the coca crop was fumigated. In 1998, no drop in the number of hectares grown. The net effect: a rise in the price of coca paste, coca planting spread out, displacement of land into the jungle.*

Dr. Vargas estimates that the coca plant and its cultivation represent only 1 % of the drug problem. Ninety-nine percent of the drug problem rests with the processing, transportation, distribution through smuggling, money laundering of the receipts, and the collateral damage that results from the criminality of these operations. Yet these don't seem to be the important priorities for government action. Apparently, fumigation of the coca plants has a higher priority for "Plan Colombia".

A writer for the FARC-EP says of the *campesinos:*

> *They are Colombians who don't have well known last names, who bunched their memories up in their backpacks and set off in search of new horizons, leaving their identities anchored to the land that was snatched from them by men who have ambition nailed to their souls. They went to the mountains and opened up the jungle looking for ways to survive. And one day, next to their corn, yucca, and plantains, they had to sow the coca leaf. This is the only way they could survive.*
>
> *The famous North American crusade and its biological and chemical war in the south of Colombia will only contribute to forcing these families to emigrate again. And the chain of production and commercialization of the coca leaf will emigrate with them ... South America is still home to 6.5 million square kilometers ripe for growing the coca leaf, and currently only 2,600 square kilometers are in use.*

Coca has been around in the Andean countries for thousands of years and Andean people have been chewing the coca leaf for as many years. It staves off hunger among the poor and helps people tolerate the high altitudes. In some Andean cultures, coca is considered a magical—even sacred plant. A legend handed down from earlier times; coca must never be sold for profit. Catastrophe will be visited upon anyone who does.

The monstrous truth is that the narco-traffickers are rich and powerful. That's why they're called "drug lords" and "kingpins". Corruption is rife. They can reach into the highest echelons of government, as recent history has shown. Even into the offices of presidents of nations.

The coca-growing *campesinos*, on the other hand, are poor and powerless. It's easy to target them.

The Andean legend may yet come to pass.

Why Prisons Don't Work

"It's my advice—anyone that has a child in difficulty—if it's at all possible, sell your house, borrow all the money you can to get adequate care—do anything rather than allow your son or daughter to ever serve a prison sentence!"

So says Ray Procunier, a former commissioner of California's prison system.

The prisons of America have been producing a tide of sociopaths that are flooding back into society, creating the greatest crime wave ever, according to criminologists who have expressed their concern about the situation.

The controversy over the effects of imprisonment has raged in this country since the Quakers invented the penitentiary in the Eighteenth Century. The theory was that a period of silence and solitude, locked up, would reform offenders.

But, the Quakers quickly learned that it didn't work. Inmates failed to become "penitent" in solitary confinement. On the contrary, most became more hostile, more abusive, more violent.

Nothing succeeds like failure. The prison system has had a healthy growth for more than two centuries. It has become more robust with age. Today, close to a million Americans are doing time in the nation's lock-ups, county jails, state penitentiaries and Federal prisons, triple the number of a decade ago. Most of them will pass through the revolving door and be back on the streets again, sooner or later.

Keeping Americans locked up in state and federal prisons is now costing the taxpayers more than $11.4 billion dollar a year, according to American Correctional Association figures for 1988. At the same time, it is churning more criminals back onto the streets than ever before.

With our high tech penitentiaries, today, with massive prison populations mingling in a confined cauldron, conditions are even more dismal
and more dangerous than when our Quaker forefathers got the idea of
making offenders penitent.

In all the years of devotion to the system, apologists for it never clearly
defined the purpose of prisons. Are they supposed to reform criminals? Or
punish them? Or just get them off the streets and out of sight for a period
of time. All three reasons have been advanced, singly and in various com-
binations, depending on the political climate. Added to these is the theory
of deterrence—the assumption that imprisonment of offenders will keep
others from committing similar crimes. A few honest people will admit to
a need for a feeling of revenge and retribution.

Prisons don't work for a number of reasons. Not the least of which is
that inmates are smarter than guards. There are a lot more of them—an
average ratio of 26 to 1. With no disrespect to correctional officers, they
are at the low end of the pay scale and the low end of the educational spec-
trum. Most state penitentiaries are tucked away in remote areas and are
staffed by locals where opportunities are limited.

Inmates, on the other hand, are mostly city slickers, and if not innately
more educated, have street smarts. When they get to prison, they can usually out-smart their keepers.

It's common practice, in almost all prisons, if not common knowledge,
that the authorities have to let the inmates run the pen. Experience shows
there is, basically, no other way to run a prison. Shrewd administrators
must know how to manipulate a prison population or they don't keep
their jobs.

Almost all prisons are run on a racket and snitch system. Honcho
inmates are allowed to run their rackets, be it drugs, booze, gambling,
prostitution (male and female), in exchange for helping the administration
keep the lid on. Criminal activity on the inside parallels criminal activity
on the outside. In many cases, it's a "joint" venture with guards, captains,
supervisors and sometimes wardens, in on the take.

Information is vital. Knowing what's going on behind the tense exterior
of inmate behavior is vital for any administrator. Intelligence gathering has

been developed into a fine art. In many cases, it is franchised to an intricate network of inmate stoolies. It is based on a reward and protection formula.

Grooming a stoolpigeon, and keeping him productive is important. A good snitch operation can cut costs in training and personnel. It's an efficient system until it breaks down as it did in the riot at the Santa Fe, New Mexico penitentiary in 1980. Thirty-three inmates were brutally murdered, most of them snitches. Most of the prison was destroyed in the riot. It cost the state over 89 million to rebuild, so it proven to be not so efficient after all.

Prisons are ideally designed for corruption. The opportunities for bribery, embezzlement, fraud and outright theft are mammoth. State legislatures tend to sweep correctional problems under the rug. Perhaps, because their constituents want it that way. Nobody likes to face and deal with matters that are unpleasant and frightening. There is a paucity of accountability when it comes to running prisons. Responsibility is passed to underlings and so on down the line. Lower levels of management, those who must deal directly with inmates, take on the onus. That's where the joint ventures begin.

Prisons distill racism. For some reason, the cauldron of the penitentiary cooks up all the racial feelings of both solidarity and hate that exist in society and magnifies it. It's a need for belonging. It's a requirement for survival. Prison gangs more than parallel gangs on the street. In many ways they are the breeding grounds and feeders for the street gang structure on the outside, be it the Black Muslims, the Mexican Mafia or the Aryan Brotherhood..

If prisons are schools for crime, than most students have been well taught. One young man doing time for murder, committed two more while in prison. In a moment of self revelation, he described his incorrigible nature on the outside. But, in prison, he allowed, he had become a monster.

Virulent racism … unbridled corruption … intolerable violations of the human spirit … bankrupt theories of rehabilitation … unacceptable social costs … is this the heritage of America's prison system?

If prisons are that evil an institution, what if, in a flash, all prisons could be abolished from this earth, what would we do with all the criminals? The armed robbers, the drug pushers, the rapists, the arsonists, the murderers?

Most would be out there on the street where they are now. Even under our present system, it is estimated that only 10% of those committing crimes are caught, and of these, less than 2% convicted of a felony, ever spend time in prison.

Alternatives to prison have been tried but have never been given a fair chance in this country. Scandinavian countries have made the most progress in a more humane penology where offenders have been treated in a variety of community-based alternatives.

Even our most radical penologists do not propose the total abolition of prisons, but many suggest a more rational form of treatment. It is estimated by some that only 10% of those in medium or maximum security prisons need to be there. The rest can be controlled, with as much safety for society, in community based programs.

Experience with intensive probation (drastically reduced caseloads) has already proven to be extremely effective. This, coupled with more extensive use of parole supervision, smaller and more controlled group homes and halfway houses for juvenile offenders, are some of the substitutes for prison that can be developed, at a fraction of the cost. But, even the slightest movement toward a more liberal policy, prison furloughs and work release programs, has been dealt a hard blow by the "Willie Horton syndrome".

With 45% of the criminal justice bureaucracy now glutted with drug-related crime, new approaches are needed in the entire criminal justice system. A good start would be a reconsideration of penalties for victim-less crime. But on this, and other aspects of the problem, very little new thinking can be expected from the Bush Administration.

TEX—A Short Story—1949

There are some people you can read like a book and there are some people you just can't figure. Take that fellow, Tex, for example. He was a strange one. I thought I understood people until I came up against him. I never could figure what made him tick the way he did.

His name was Alvin Downs but the boys over in first assembly used to call him Tex because he always wore those high-heeled cowboy boots. He was a little skinny guy but strong and wiry for his size, young, about 25 I'd say but with one of them mean looks on his face all the time that made him seem old. You know what I mean—pinched and dried up and like he never had anything that was enjoyable to think about.

He never had much to do with anyone in the plant but he took a shine to me after a while and I guess I became his unofficial friend after we'd been workin' side by side for a month or two.

"You know," he told me one day, "I don't have to be doin' this work."

"No?" I asked.

Naw … my pop's got a ranch down in Texas. A great big ranch with lots and lots of lan.' Cotton lan,' too. And that's a good payin' crop. I could be down there now runnin' the farm. Not much work. Sit on the porch and watch them niggers work …"

He'd tell me that story not once, but maybe two, three times a day—whenever he'd get to day dreaming real hard. The way he'd pound those rivets while his mind would spin that story, I could see his pappy was no ranch-owner but probably a leatherneck dirt farmer and that he had learned to use a hammer as soon as he was old enough to hold one.

I only began to learn the meanness there was in Tex when the old colored woman who worked for the tag factory down the street had an accident on the streetcar. From the way I heard the story it was an open and shut case of negligence by the conductor. Tex happened to be on the car.

He had such a damned streak of meanness he volunteered to go down to court and testify it was the colored woman's fault. He got time off from work with pay and a little bonus on the side from the streetcar company. But it wasn't just the money that pleased Tex so damned much. He wore a big grin around the plant for two days afterward shooting his mouth off how he kept that woman from getting any compensation.

I used to try to find out what Tex did nights after work. But I couldn't get much out of him. He wasn't married. He didn't have a girl that I knew of. At least, he never mentioned one. When I'd pump him about his private life he'd talk vaguely about all the women he had but he never tried to sound convincing.

Every night, he ate at the cafeteria where he used to work when he first came to Los Angeles. He started there as a bus-boy at twenty-nine a week and meals and had worked himself up to third chef before he left to take the job at the factory. After four years, he couldn't break his eating habits so he always went back to the cafeteria for his dinner.

He lived in a rented room not far from the factory, but our friendship ended when the five o'clock whistle blew so I wouldn't know what kind of home he had. As far as I know, he had no friends, he didn't belong to any clubs and he never went to the movies.

But all this isn't the hard thing to understand about Tex. There are lots of people that fit into a pattern like that. It was what I learned later that baffled me.

Things were building up to a showdown at the plant. Our union contract was running out, the bosses were out to break the union and it looked like strike.

We had a bunch of weak sisters in the shop and Tex was one of them. We had tried for months to sign him up but all he'd tell us was that he didn't believe in unions.

"Every man for himself—" he'd say if you tried to talk union to him. No one's goin' ta look after me but me—"

The fact that he was getting the union minimum of a dollar thirty-seven and a half an hour, that it had taken the union a lot of time and a lot of blood to win, didn't cut any ice with Tex.

Soon as he got wind of what was up he high-tailed it to Glenn, the superintendent and pledged allegiance. He promised to come to work no matter what and the hell with what the union said. For this, Glenn promised to jack his pay up to a dollar sixty an hour, top wage in the plant, and that applied to anyone else who came to work after June 30th, the day our contract ran out.

We knew it would be tough going but there was no choice. The bosses sat it out and let the contract lapse. July 1, we hit the bricks.

It was a great line that first day. The local downtown sent up reinforcements and we had three hundred pickets on the street. The plant shut down tighter'n a crunk on a three-day binge.

The spirit of the men was high and even the rats among us stopped to think it over twice. But not Tex. He came out like a fighting cock and wanted through. Some of the boys, figuring him for a green punk kid, tried to reason with him, but I could've told them to save their breath. Tex plunged the line like a quarterback in scrimmage. He got thrown for a loss and when they un-piled he was on the bottom.

The next morning, Tex was back. At the regular starting time, he was at the gate. But the line had beaten him there. This time, he drove right up in his thirty-nine Chevvie and on a signal, Glenn, on the inside, opened the gate for him to drive through.

He jazzed the motor, shouted a few threats and headed the Chevvie into the line. But before he got more than a few feet we were over the car like a swarm of locust. We dragged Tex out and I tried to keep him from getting hurt too bad. Meanwhile, the boys were playing teeter-totter with the Chevvie. The thing that brought tears to Tex's eyes was not the pummeling he got but the sight of his old car on its side like a dead bug.

Anyway, they turned his car and that was the beginning of the end. The rest followed in its usual sequence. The old vaudeville act. First, the Sheriff's boys arrived, that impartial group of gallant young men whose job it is to preserve law and order, who mete out the law with equal justice to both sides. They read the riot act and quick as you could say Jack Robinson they had the injunction out. Four pickets allowed. Two at each gate. The rest of us had to hug the opposite curb.

Glenn was no slouch. He worked it so they brought a load of steel in that afternoon. We razzed the teamster as he eased the truck up to the yard gate. I could see the conflict rage somewhere in the driver's mind, but somebody higher up must have given him a little lecture on union policy and there was too much job insecurity, selfishness and ignorance to tip the scales the other way.

Tex and a handful of other scabs that crossed the first day spent the afternoon in the yard unloading the truck in full view of the rest of us across the street.

Joe Sugars, a punch press operator, stood next to me at the curb. Without taking his eyes from the men working on the truck, he spat into the gutter.

"Thirteen years I put into that plant. I saw the union come. Look at them bastards!"

For the next few weeks it was touch and go. Except for about a dozen finks all the men held firm. The bosses couldn't stand the production losses and for a while it looked as though they'd yield. But meanwhile they were bringing through a few men every day. Men who hadn't learned to be men. Young punks from out of town. Poor whites fresh from the South. A hand-picked crop of union-busters if ever there was one.

It was the injunction and the Sheriff's men that killed us finally. We had no way of stopping the scabs from crossing through. In a couple of months they had us licked. It was all over except for the grim little legal picket line.

I sat out a few months of unemployment and then got a job in a shop not far from the old plant. I was in a lunch joint having a sandwich one day when out of the corner of my eye I saw Tex coming through the door. I tried to avoid his glance but he saw me and came over and sat down on the next stool.

"Howdy," he said and chucked me on the back with a bony paw. I acknowledged his presence with a half hearted nod and went on eating my sandwich.

"What's the matter? Don't you say hello to an old friend," Tex went on cheerfully.

"Still drawing down your dollar sixty an hour, Tex?" I asked.

He gave me his snaggle tooth grin. "You ain't still sore 'bout that?" he said. "You got no right to kick. You workin' agin. Besides, what's that got to do with me? I'm lookin' out for myself. No one else goin' to. That damn union—all they do is spoil a fella's job. Them pickets beat me up. Turn my car over. The hell with them."

I tried to tell Tex he was cutting his own throat. They were taking on men at the plant now for ninety cents an hour and less. They wouldn't keep him long.

"They turn my car over," was all he said.

I didn't see Tex again for a long time after that. About six months passed and I lost my job again—on a lay-off. Times were getting tough. I was down at the unemployment office picking up my check the other day, and who do I run into standing in the line but Tex.

This time I greeted him with a slap on the back. Tex didn't look too happy now.

"So they finally gave you the ax," I said without trying to hide my feelings.

"Naw, he muttered, "things were slowin' up. They had to let me go."

That was all he said.

I waited for Tex to pick up his check, met him at the door and went out with him.

"I know where I can get me a good job," he said when we were on the street. "There's a strike over at Century. Takin' on men for a dollar six-bits. Fella tole me …"

I left Tex standing on the corner. After a while he clomped off on his cowboy boots.

What are you goin' to do with a guy like that?

Where Is Trotsky?

The battle of the century is the one that raged in Russia before and during the Bolshevik Revolution of 1917. The antagonists were Leon Trotsky and Vladimir Lenin and after Lenin's death in 1924, Joseph Stalin took up the cudgels (literally) against Trotsky that finally ended in Mexico with an ax in Trotsky's head.

The substance of the disagreement, to use a mild term, between Lenin and Trotsky and later Stalin and Trotsky was whether socialism could be successfully established in one country surrounded by capitalist nations—or could socialism only be achieved through world revolution.

Trotsky felt that the capitalist nations would strangle a fledgling socialist regime in the cradle. Lenin didn't think most countries in the capitalist world were ready for socialism. Toward the end of World War I and the fall of the Czarist regime, Russia was ripe for the taking, so why not take it? The Bolsheviks pulled it off when they overthrew the provisional government of Kerensky. So Lenin and Stalin won the argument. The Soviet Union was established—a Soviet Socialist island in a sea of capitalism.

After Lenin's death, Stalin hunkered down and turned the Soviet Union into "fortress socialism". Socialism had a tough time in forty some years of the Cold War, but in one form or another it stayed alive. Other forms evolved in a few countries, China and Cuba being notable examples. By 1989, the walls came tumbling down. The Soviet system ran out of steam. A country without a democratic tradition, isolated and encircled by capitalist nations, a country that tried to pull itself up by its own economic bootstraps, eventually collapsed of its own bureaucratic weight. Could it be that Trotsky was right?

After World War II, capitalism was riding high. The road was open to conglomerate building. The drive to maximize profits took off.

Well, half a century later here we are. The millenium. The conglomerates are conglomerated. Check any field. The Bells. SBC Communications and Ameritech, NYNEX and Bell Atlantic, long lines and local service. Cable and Internet. Toll roads on the information superhighway. Time Warner and Turner Broadcasting. ABC and Disney. CBS and Westinghouse. Hard news and hardened missile sites. Microsoft and NBC and General Electric. Nike swooshes the world. Banks, insurance and financial services. Smith Barney and Salomon Brothers, Citicorp and Travelers. Automobiles. Daimler-Benz and Chrysler. Rolls Royce and Volkswagen. Pharmaceuticals and HMOs. ADM—supermarket to the world. It goes on and on. Hundreds of billions and billions of dollars. Mergers and acquisitions and takeovers take off. A snowball rolling down hill. The expanding universe of monopoly. The globe has been globalized.

The wealth of the world trickles up into the hands of a precious few. Will one mega-transnational corporate conglomerate eventually own everything? When it comes to that will the people of the world have the power to take it over? The big bang. World revolution. Viola! Socialism.

Where is Trotsky now that we really need him?

Curb the Corporations

There are people and there are dogs. There are people and there are corporations. Corporations should have the status of dogs. They must be curbed.

You wouldn't let your dog run around loose relieving himself whenever and wherever he wants—or biting people. You'd obedience train him and teach him to behave. A proper pet learns to live in a people's world.

Corporations are our pet projects—collections of productive capacity—tools designed by people and made to serve people. They make our clothes and food and shelter and the things we need for a better life.

When we kicked out the British Imperial companies after our Revolution, we tried to make sure that our own companies would not do what the British companies had done, rob and cheat the people. Safeguards were built into the constitutions of the several States. Limited liability companies, now called "corporations" had to obtain charters from the State to do business. There are rules and regulations. They are chartered to do a specific job. If they don't do the job or break the rules, their charters can be revoked. The State giveth and the State can taketh away. That's the way the system was set up in the States' constitutions. And this charter system is still in force in most states.

But, alas ... who remembers? Early in the 19th Century, when this country was young and still wet behind the ears, Congress gave corporations the status of people and the corporations soon began to eat congressmen and senators and judges and politicians of all stripes, and even presidents. And they began to relieve themselves all over the place, and bite people. When the people saw what was happening, they started to fight back. The Populist Movement, in the late 19th Century, won a few battles here and there. The Progressive Party in the midwest. The Farmer-Labor Party. LaFollette in Wisconsin and Minnesota. But after a while they were whittled away by power and wealth and lost the war. By the end of the Century, the Robber Barons reigned supreme.

A hundred years later, in the 1980s the Reagan Revolution gave what was left of the store away. Deregulation. The Airlines. The Trucking Industry. The Banks. Mergers and acquisitions, the order of the day. Junk Bonds. Michael Milken. Even the FCC. No more fairness and balance necessary in TV News.

Who remembers the Sherman Act and the Clayton Act? Antitrust laws passed at the beginning of this century to mitigate the damage of the Robber Barons. All but forgotten. A feeble attempt, now and then, like the recent attempt to stop Bill Gates and Microsoft from getting a near monopoly on internet services.

It has become conventional wisdom that corporations have the attributes of people, not dogs. They can buy anything they wanted—like elections—even other countries. Not only did Congress give corporations the status of people, but only recently the Supreme Court of the United States upheld the right of freedom of speech and freedom of the press for a non-living organism! They might as well have thrown in freedom of religion. The constitution of the United States intended *human rights* for human beings!

The 1994 Presidential election and the 1996 mid-term election aptly demonstrated what effect this had. More entrenched corporate power. A campaign finance reform scandal. The selling of America's soul.

Corporations devoured the communications industry, and near total control of mass communications. Their self-serving propaganda became the main stream thinking of the nation. A major theme—government stinks—even a feeble government that might put a damper on corporate power. Dissident views and alternative opinions are shut out.

What are we going to do about it? Not much, it seems. Have you heard anyone suggesting the revocation of a few corporate charters? I haven't. Those laws are still on the books.

Corporate power leads to corporate control of government which leads to a Corporate State which is another term for fascism, or if that word frightens you call it *totalitarianism.*

The first crack in the global corporate market is showing up in the overheated economies of the newly industrialized East Asian countries. Too much productive capacity—too few consumer markets. Where are they going to dump all this stuff? How many of these countries can the US and the IMF bail out?

We're seeing massive trade deficits in the US and a spiraling deflation in the world markets. Prescription for disaster. Eventually it will come home to roost. The corporations are choking themselves. Must we wait until they do? Must we wait for the crash? This one will make the Great Depression of the Thirties look like the Mad Hatter's tea party.

It's time to leash the dog for its own good. It's time to save democracy and the capitalist system as we have known it. It's time to give the corporations some obedience training for their own good. Bring back regulation. Bring back big government with a big stick. Bring back the Sherman Act. The NRA. Roosevelt saved them once, despite themselves. Maybe it can be done again.

Let's leash the dog before it's too late. Heel.

PART III
Afterword

Who I Am

Stephen Fleischman's career as a documentary writer-director-producer spans more than three decades—10 years with CBS NEWS, 20 years with ABC NEWS—independent documentary production and writing for television.

His final program for ABC NEWS was THE COCAINE CARTEL, a one-hour investigative report for the CLOSEUP series. He took a film crew to Medellin, Colombia, the cocaine capitol of the world. The program named and reported on the five largest and most dangerous drug traffickers. When THE COCAINE CARTEL aired on the ABC Network it sent shock waves through the drug world from Miami to Bogotá.

Fleischman began his television career at CBS NEWS as writer and story editor in 1953. He worked with Irving Gitlin's Public Affairs unit on the award-winning series, THE SEARCH, an examination of research projects at America's leading universities. He was then named producer of the children's program, LET'S TAKE A TRIP, hosted by Sonny Fox, which gained wide acclaim. He went on to produce THE AMERICAN CHALLENGE with Eric Severeid as host—and in 1957–58 was producer of hour-long special programs in Walter Cronkite's THE TWENTIETH CENTURY series that captured a number of EMMY AWARDS.

In 1959, Fleischman participated in the formation of the renowned Murrow-Friendly CBS REPORTS series. Fleischman's first assignment as Producer-Director was NIGERIA—THE FREEDOM EXPLOSION, a program that chronicled the birth of that nation in 1960. It won an OVERSEAS PRESS CLUB AWARD for Fleischman and Eric Severeid, the correspondent on the program.

Fleischman continued to write, produce and direct CBS REPORTS programs for the next five years. They included THE BUSINESS OF HEALTH: MONEY, MEDICINE AND POLITICS with Correspondent Howard K. Smith, a scrutiny of the controversies that raged around the health care issues of the time. Fleischman's BIRTH CONTROL AND THE LAW won the coveted <u>ALBERT AND MARY LASKER MEDICAL JOURNALISM AWARD</u> for 1962. It was the first program of its kind to deal candidly, and in depth, with the social, moral and legal controversies over birth control and the new FDA-approved birth control pill. CBS REPORTS: THE HARLEM TEMPER, in 1963, was the first treatment of the rising Black Nationalist movement with extensive coverage of the role of Malcolm X.

In 1964, ABC NEWS President, Elmer Lower, brought Fleischman to the burgeoning News Division of the American Broadcasting Companies where Fleischman established his own Documentary Unit.

For the next ten years, as Producer and Executive Producer, he turned out three to four one-hour and two-hour specials a year that won a number of awards. In 1964, THE GREAT DIVIDE: CIVIL RIGHTS AND THE BILL caught the turmoil of the Civil Rights struggle of the time. That year, he also produced MAN INVADES THE SEA, with the participation of Astronaut Scott Carpenter and WE ARE NOT ALONE with New York Times Science Reporter, Walter Sullivan.

With the escalation of the Vietnam War in1965, Fleischman went to Vietnam with Correspondent Edward P. Morgan to produce a documentary on our role there. The result was a one hour program entitled THE AGONY OF VIETNAM. When telecast in August of 1965 it raised a storm of controversy—hailed by anti-war forces for its objectivity, criticized in government circles because it did support US policy on the war.

Fleischman continued to produce documentaries dealing with science and medicine, cultural and social themes. The year 1966 saw the beginning of a series of four hour-long documentaries on American music, the first of which was THE ANATOMY OF POP: THE MUSIC EXPLOSION. It has had repeated telecasts on the ABC Network and in syndication. In that year, as a special request of ABC Board Chairman, Leonard Goldenson, Fleischman was asked to produce a Public Service program on the subject of retardation in children. THE LONG CHILDHOOD OF TIMMY was the result. The program focused on the personal story of a

Downs Syndrome child and his loving family. It won Fleischman a second
<u>LASKER MEDICAL JOURNALISM AWARD.</u>

The years 1969 and 1970 saw the dawning, in the American conscious-
ness, of pollution problems threatening this country. In those years, Fleischman produced a three-part series called MISSION POSSIBLE and a
two-hour special, THREE YOUNG AMERICANS IN SEARCH OF
SURVIVAL, narrated by Paul Newman, on the subject of ecological and
environmental problems. They were the first in-depth studies of this subject on network television. In 1970, another corporate request, an ABC
NEWS gift to UNICEF, was assigned to Fleischman. The documentary
special TO ALL THE WORLD'S CHILDREN, took him to three conti-
nents, to Paraguay, to Kenya and to Sri Lanka (Ceylon) to show
UNICEF's work in the context of national and cultural influences on children. The program is narrated by film actor Rod Steiger and is still in exhi-
bition at the UN.

*By 1973, the ABC NEWS commitment to the television documentary took
another leap.*

The individual production units were merged into ABC NEWS CLO-
SEUP, a regularly scheduled monthly documentary series under the aegis
of Av Westin. Fleischman continued to function as writer-director-producer on the series for the next ten years.

Some of his notable contributions—WEST VIRGINIA: LIFE, LIB-
ERTY AND THE PURSUIT OF COAL, the premiere program, broke
new ground in setting the form and style for the series. It garnered an
<u>EMMY AWARD</u> for CLOSEUP. The following year OIL: THE POL-
ICY CRISIS with Correspondent Brit Hume brought a different view-
point to the so-called "energy crisis" of 1974. In that year, too, CLOSEUP
ON HOFFA, an investigative biography with unusual access to the man,
sharpened the focus on Jimmy Hoffa, Frank Fitzsimmons, the Teamsters'
Union and its connections to government and organized crime. It was
cited for excellence in investigative reporting.

In 1975, Fleischman's investigative report, THE CIA, anticipated the
conclusions of the highly critical Rockefeller Commission findings that

were released later that year. Other investigative reports on consumerism and fraud followed.

The 1979 NEW YORK STATE BROADCASTERS AWARD went to Fleischman's NOBODY'S CHILDREN, a penetrating revelation of foster care and adoption scandals in New York, Chicago and New Orleans.

In the 1980's, Fleischman produced documentaries on penology, science and politics, and another program on the United Nations, its peace-keeping and refugee relief missions. This took him to the refugee camps in Honduras and to the firing line with UNIFIL troops in Lebanon in 1982, on the eve of the Israeli invasion of that country.

Fleischman's career at ABC NEWS was capped in 1983 with the prestigious COLUMBIA UNIVERSITY-DUPONT TELEVISION JOURNALISM AWARD for his CLOSEUP: THE GENE MERCHANTS. This was the first television exploration of DNA and the new science of gene splicing and its ethical and economic ramifications for society.

In the later part of the 80's, Fleischman worked with Yue-Sai Kan, Executive Producer and Host of the cable television series LOOKING EAST. The programs, aired on the SPN cable network, were designed to convey a better understanding of the Far East to American audiences. Miss Kan was also awarded a contract by CCTV, the television network of the People's Republic of China, to produce 52 15-minute programs to explain the rest of the world to Chinese audiences. Fleischman, who traveled with Miss Kan and a videotape crew to South America and Europe, wrote and directed a number of these programs. The series, entitled ONE WORLD, was dubbed in Mandarin and English and both versions were telecast twice throughout the People's Republic before the Tienanmen Square events of 1989.

In recent years, Fleischman has devoted himself to writing fiction and non-fiction, much of it based on his experiences in network news. Forty of Mr. Fleischman's documentaries are in the collection and archives of THE MUSEUM OF TELEVISION AND RADIO in New York and Los Angeles.

Stephen Fleischman is a member of the Directors Guild of America, Inc. and a *Lifetime Current Member* of the Writers Guild of America, East, Inc. He is a graduate of *Haverford College*, Class of 1940, with a Bachelor of Arts degree and is presently living in Los Angeles with his wife, Dede Allen, a life-long feature film editor.

Documentography

The documentaries of Stephen Fleischman in the collection and archives of The Paley Center for Media (formerly the Museum of Television and Radio) available for screening in New York and Beverly Hills.

1. **CORNELL: AUTO SAFETY RESEARCH** 1953 (black and white) one half hour with Walter Cronkite *THE SEARCH* series
   CBS NEWS Public Affairs

2. **ARKANSAS: FOLKLORE RESEARCH** 1954 (black and white) one half hour with Charles Romaine *THE SEARCH* series
   CBS NEWS Public Affairs

3. **THE FACE OF CRIME** 1958 (black and white) one hour with Walter Cronkite *THE TWENTIETH CENTURY* series
   CBS NEWS Public Affairs

4. **GENERATION WITHOUT A CAUSE** 1959
   Part 1 *Self Portrait* (black and white) one half hour
   Part 2 *The Searchers* (black and white) one half hour
   THE TWENTIETH CENTURY series with Walter Cronkite
   CBS NEWS Public Affairs

5. **NIGERIA: THE FREEDOM EXPLOSION** 1960 (black and white) one hour with Eric Sevareid
   CBS Reports, CBS NEWS

6. **THE GREAT FARM VOTE OF '63** 1963 (black and white one hour with Harry Reasoner
   CBS Reports, CBS NEWS

7. **THE GREAT DIVIDE: CIVIL RIGHTS AND THE BILL** 1964 (black and white) onehour with Bob Young
   ABC NEWS DOCUMENTARY UNIT

8. **JFK: HIS TWO WORLDS** 1964 (black & white) one hour with Bill Downs, Bill Lawrence and Edward P. Morgan
   ABC NEWS DOCUMENTARY UNIT

9. **THE AGONY OF VIETNAM** 1965 (black & white) one hour with Edward P. Morgan
   ABC NEWS DOCUMENTARY UNIT

10. **MAN INVADES THE SEA** 1965 (black and white) one hour with Robert Montgomery
ABC NEWS DOCUMENTARY UNIT

11. **EVERYBODY'S GOT A SYSTEM** 1965 (black and white) one hour with Terry Thomas.
ABC NEWS DOCUMENTARY UNIT

12. **ANATOMY OF POP:** The Music Explosion 1966 (black and white) one-hour with Bob Young
ABC NEWS DOCUMENTARY UNIT

13. **THE BAFFLING WORLD OF ESP** 1966 (black and white) one hour with Basil Rathbone
ABC NEWS DOCUMENTARY UNIT

14. **WE ARE NOT ALONE** 1966 (black and white) one hour with *NEW YORK TIMES* Science
Editor, Walter Sullivan
ABC NEWS DOCUMENTARY UNIT

15. **THE LONG CHILDHOOD OF TIMMY** 1966 (black and white) one hour with E.G. Marshall
ABC NEWS DOCUMENTARY UNIT

16. **RIDDLE OF THE MAYAN CAVE** 1967 (black and white) one hour with the EXPLORERS CLUB
ABC NEWS DOCUMENTARY UNIT

17. **ONE NIGHT STANDS** 1967 (color) (Woody Herman's Herd, Johnny Rivers, the Bartok Circus) one hour with Bing Crosby
ABC NEWS DOCUMENTARY UNIT

18. **THE SONG MAKERS** 1968 (color) one hour with Narrator Joel Crager
ABC NEWS DOCUMENTARY UNIT

19. **THE SINGERS** 1969 (color) one hour with Gloria Loring and Aretha Franklin
ABC NEWS DOCUMENTARY UNIT

20. **ATLANTA: It Can Be Done** 1969 (color) one hour
ABC NEWS DOCUMENTARY UNIT

21. **BLACK FIDDLER: Prejudice and the Negro** 1969 (color) one hour
ABC NEWS DOCUMENTARY UNIT

22. **THREE YOUNG AMERICANS IN SEARCH OF SURVIVAL 1969** (color) two hours
with Paul Newman
ABC NEWS DOCUMENTARY UNIT

23. **TO ALL THE WORLD'S CHILDREN** 1970 (color) one hour for UNICEF with Rod Steiger
ABC NEWS DOCUMENTARY UNIT

24. **MISSION POSSBLE: Part One** *They Care For A City* 1970 (San Francisco) (color) one hour with Colonel Frank Borman
ABC NEWS DOCUMENTARY UNIT

25. **MISSION POSSBLE: Part Two** *They Care for the Land* 1969 (color) one hour with Colonel Frank Borman
ABC NEWS DOCUMENTART UNIT

26. **MISSION POSSBLE: Part Three** *They Care For A Nation* 1970 (color) one hour with Colonel Frank Borman
ABC NEWS DOCUMENTARY UNIT

27. **THE CHEROKEE SHAFT: The Story of Mines and Men** 1971 (color) one hour with Frank Reynolds
ABC NEWS DOCUMENTARY UNIT

28. **ASSAULT ON PRIVACY** 1972 (color) one hour with Frank Reynolds
ABC NEWS DOCUMENTARY UNIT

29. **OCEANS: The Silent Crisis** 1972 (color) one hour
ABC NEWS DOCUMENTARY UNIT

30. **THE YOUNG CONVICTS: Prison in the Streets** 1972 (color) one hour with Frank Reynolds
ABC NEWS DOCUMENTARY UNIT

31. **THE BUILDING INNOVATORS** 1973 (color) one hour with Frank Reynolds
ABC NEWS DOCUMENTARY UNIT

32. **WEST VIRGINIA: LIFE, LIBERTY AND THE PURSUIT OF COAL 1973** (color) one hour with Jim Kincaid and Brit Hume
ABC NEWS CLOSEUP

33. **HOFFA** 1974 (color) one hour An investigative biography of former Teamster President James R. Hoffa with Jim Kincaid, Bill Gill and Brit Hume
ABC NEWS CLOSEUP

34. **MEDICINE AND MONEY** 1976 (color) one hour with Frank Reynolds
ABC NEWS CLOSEUP

35. **ERA: The War Between the Women** 1977 (color) one hour with Howard K. Smith
ABC NEWS CLOSEUP

36. **NOBODY'S CHILDREN** 1979 (color) one hour with Brit Hume
ABC NEWS CLOSEUP

37. **DEATH IN A SOUTHWEST PRISON** 1980 (color) one hour with Tom Jarrell
ABC NEWS CLOSEUP

38. **THE GENE MERCHANTS** 1981 (color) one hour with Marshall Frady
ABC NEWS CLOSEUP

39. **THE COCAINE CARTEL** 1983 (color) one hour with Bill Redeker
ABC NEWS CLOSEUP

40. **PRISON GROUP THERAPY** (Bordentown Reformatory, New Jersey) Supplement to
THE TWENTIETH CENTURY series special *The Face of Crime* 1958 (black and white)
two hours
CBS NEWS

978-0-595-46445-6
0-595-46445-9